Messerschmitt Me 262

Arrow to the Future

Messerschmitt Me 262

Arrow to the Future

By WALTER J. BOYNE

Published for the
NATIONAL AIR AND SPACE MUSEUM

By the
SMITHSONIAN INSTITUTION PRESS

Washington, D.C.

Printed in the United States of America

LIBRARY OF CONGRESS CATALOGING IN PUBLICATION DATA
Boyne, Walter J   1929–
    Messerschmitt Me 262.
    Bibliography: p.
    1.   Messerschmitt Me 262 (Fighter planes)   I.   Title.
UG1242.F5B69   358.4′3   80–607090
ISBN 0–87474–276–5
ISBN 0–87474–275–7 (pbk.)

Unless otherwise noted, photographs are from the National Air and Space Museum.

Fully detailed plans are available from:
    Ken Bokelman
    7735 Pickering #20
    Whittier, CA 90602

Contents

Foreword

GENERALLEUTNANT ADOLF GALLAND

The Me 262 was not the first jet aircraft to fly, but it was the first to be employed operationally in wartime service. Military and civil aircraft up to that time were powered by piston engines driving propellers, whereas the Messerschmitt utilized a completely different means of propulsion. Virtually nobody at that time realized that a totally new epoch in aviation had begun.

When I first saw and test-flew the Me 262 proto-type—then a well-kept secret—at Augsburg on 22 May 1943, I was extraordinarily impressed. Remembering that day and the sensational feeling I got flying the plane, I was moved to make the following statement: "It is as if an angel were pushing."

I was immediately convinced that the revolutionary new Me 262 could fly at least 100 knots faster than any Allied fighter aircraft. It offered us a remarkable chance. As a matter of fact, this jet airplane was the single best answer to the steadily increasing and overwhelming air superiority of the Allies on the Western Front.

On 25 May 1943, I submitted the following brief report to *Feldmarschall* Erhard Milch, who was responsible at that time for *Luftwaffe* development, testing, and production:

Dear *Feldmarschall*,

On Saturday the 22nd, I flight-tested the Me 262 in Augsburg. I would like to state the following:
1. The aircraft is a trump card which will guarantee us an unbelievable advantage during operations, if the enemy keeps flying piston-engine aircraft.
2. From a pilot's standpoint, the flight performance is quite impressive.
3. The engines are satisfactory, except during takeoff and landing.
4. The aircraft will provide us with revolutionary new tactical opportunities.

I cordially request that you recommend the following:
a) stop Me 209 production
b) concentrate the total piston fighter production capacity on the Fw 190 with the BMW 801 engine, and the Fw 190 with either the DB 603 or Jumo 213 engines
c) have the development and production capacity thereby freed devoted immediately to the Me 262 program.

When the Me 262 was presented to Hitler in December, 1943, he decided that this superlative fighter airplane should be operated only as a *"Blitzbomber"* or fast bomber.

No other major development in aviation, or in the entire field of weapon systems, has ever elicited so much drama and poor judgment. This is why the approximately 1,400 Me 262 aircraft produced brought about no decisive success, either as a fighter or bomber.

It can be taken as a certainty that only 300 Me 262s would have caused unbearable losses to the B-17s and B-24s of the USAAF, or that the American strategic bombardment offensive would have been completely halted.

The free world should be very grateful to the National Air and Space Museum for the oustanding restoration of a Messerschmitt Me 262, and to Walter J. Boyne for his excellent book on this plane.

Acknowledgments

It is difficult to list everyone who has helped me in this venture. My heart-felt thanks goes to Jay Spenser, my colleague and friend and a fine writer and researcher. I also want to thank Woldemar Voigt, who spent many hours reviewing the text and provided fascinating insights into an engineer's life in the Third Reich, and who passed away on June 20, 1980.

A special mention must go to Dolf Lehmann, and the members of the *Luftwaffe* and the Society of German Fighter Pilots who responded to my questionnaire and to Colonel Peter Jungmichel, Air Attache of the Federal Republic of Germany, who coordinated their responses. *Generalleutnant* Adolf Galland was especially helpful as were *Generalmajor* Erich Hohagen, *Hauptmann* Ernest Maison, *Major* Rudolph Sinner, *Generalleutnant* Johannes Steinhoff, *Oberst* Gerd Stamp, *Generalmajor* Walter Windisch, and many others.

I owe much to:

Ken Bokelman, draftsman, Dr. Ludwig Bolkow, engineer, Warren Bodie, Peter M. Bowers, the Boeing Company, J. M. Bruce, Royal Air Force Museum, Roy W. Brown, pilot, Ed Chalkley, Silver Hill, Dustin Carter, AAHS, Phil Edwards, NASM Library, Jeffery Ethell, author, Dr. Anselm Franz, engineer, Royal Frey, Curator of the Air Force Museum, Thomas J. Hitchcock, publisher, Brigader General Benjamin Kelsey, USAF (Retired), Lindbergh Scholar NASM, Felix Lowe, Smithsonian Institution, Donald S. Lopez, NASM, Harvey Lippincott, United Technology, Mike Lyons, Silver Hill, Jay Miller, Aerophile, Ed Maloney, Planes of Fame Museum, Robert C. Mikesh, NASM, Heinz Nowarra, historian, Claudia Oakes, NASM, Dr. Hans von Ohain, engineer, Messers P. Polster and H. J. Ebert, the Deutches Museum, P. M. Ryan, Australian War Memorial, J. R. Smith, author, Richard C.Seeley, publisher, Terezia Takacs, NASM, Major General Harold E. Watson, USAF (Retired), John Underwood, author, Vivian White, Air Force Museum, Charles Worman, Air Force Museum, Bess DeBeck and Janet Stratton, Smithsonian Institution, Helen McMahon, NASM, and many others.

In closing, I want to thank Toni Smith and Nancy Harris for masterminding the typing and Hernan Otano for his work with the fascinating "word processor".

Washington, DC
March, 1982

WALTER J. BOYNE

Messerschmitt Me 262

Arrow to the Future

The Messerschmitt Me 262

Good in-flight photos taken of the Me 262 during wartime are rare. This is the first Me 262 A-1 to fall into American hands, being surrendered at Rhein Main Airdrome by its Messerschmitt test pilot, Hans Fay. It is being flown here by then Major Russ Schleeh at Wright Field, Ohio, just after the war. (Courtesy Fred Johnsen)

The Messerschmitt Me 262 jet fighter burst from cloud laden German skies like a singing sword, flashing through enemy formations with a performance that at first defied belief. Long expected by Allied intelligence, and long desired by the ebbing Luftwaffe's fighter pilots, the 262 ushered in an entirely new era in air warfare.

When the *Schwalbe* (Swallow)[1] first appeared in combat in April 1944, the air war over Europe seemed settled. Endless phalanxes of B-17's and B-24's moved across the sky in stately box formations, contested almost solely by black bursts of flak. Shining silver, because with the German fighter force completely defeated they no longer needed camouflage, the big bombers were protected by ceaseless relays of Mustang, Lightning and Thunderbolt fighters.

Occasionally a gaggle of tired Messerschmitt Bf 109's or Focke Wulfe Fw-190's would slash in to try to pick off a straggler, provoking yips of joy over the radios from confident American fighter pilots swarming to the attack.

The 262 threatened to change all that. It would attack in a wide sweeping curve, so swift as to be able to climb through the formations faster than the attacking Mustangs could speed in level flight.

The *Schwalbe's* looks were as formidable as its performance; a sleek, low wing twin engine monoplane, its fuselage had a triangular shark shape which gave it an ominous beauty. It was unmistakable in the air, for it flew faster than anything around, and it had an arrow shape never seen before.

Initial contacts with the Me 262 presented the Allied commanders with some severe concerns. If some unforeseeable military development permitted Germany to introduce the aircraft in quantity, an entirely new air game plan would have to be created. The immediate response was intense bombing of factories known to be

1. Mr. Richard Smith, a distinguished historian and author has written me that despite its common use, there is no documentary evidence to prove that *Schwalbe* was ever officially used for the Me 262. Adolf Hitler approved the much more warlike *Sturmvogel* (Stormbird). For clarity, however, I have maintained conventional usage in this book, calling the fighter version *Schwalbe* and the fighter bomber *Sturmvogel*. (Adolf Galland confirms that German pilots did not use the term *Schwalbe*.)

The sleek triangular shark-like fuselage of the Me 262 was strictly functional. The landing gear, which retracted inward, was too thick for storage within the wing, so the fuselage was widened to streamline what otherwise would have been an unacceptable "bulge" in the airfoil. This is the Me 262 V6, (VI + AA) which had for the first time a fully retractable tricycle landing gear. (Courtesy Messerschmitt-Boelkow-Blohm (MBB)

producing the aircraft, and constant attempts to suppress the airfields from which it operated.

As the months wore on, Me 262 activity built slowly; attacks which had been conducted singly were soon conducted by flights of nine, twelve, and on rare occasions even 24 or 36 of the swift jets. Yet the attitude of the Allied pilots never changed. They wanted combat more than anything else, and if there were no 190's to mix it up with, then the 262 would serve perfectly well. The entire tone of the combat reports of the time reflect this lust for combat, as we shall see in Chapter Five.

The history of air combat reveals that there is usually a rough parity in fighter aircraft; thus the Fokker D. VII and Spad XIII were fair opponents in the first World War, as were the Focke Wulf Fw-190 and Spitfire Mk IX in the second World War, the North American F-86 and Mig 15 in the Korean War, and even the Mig 21 and McDonnell Douglas F-4 in the Vietnam conflict. The quantum leap of performance of the 262 over all contemporary aicraft was remarkable; a similar gain was not seen until the emergence of the Boeing XB-47 bomber in 1947, or the disclosure of the existence of the Lockheed SR-71 Blackbird in the 1960's.

There is a mystique about the *Schwalbe* that derives from its lethal beauty and its brilliant performance under circumstances of almost incredible adversity. The Me 262 was clearly at least three years ahead of its time, and its whistling jets and swept wing conveyed a spirit of the future that completely transcended the inevitably tragic role it was to have in the war.

The romance of the Me 262 is enhanced by the long standing myth that but for Hitler's bumbling incompetence, it would have been in service a year earlier than its 1944 operational debut, and that it would have swept Allied day bombers from the sky, possibly changing the course of the war, or at the least permitting exhausted Germany a negotiated peace. Such speculation is profitless, for the entire force of the Me 262 program was but a dust mote in the furious avalanche of Allied power.

The myth does a disservice to this remarkable airplane, which should be viewed entirely on its own merits; for what it was, not for what it might have been. "What if" scenarios can be written for every war, every battle, every weapon, and any desired answer can be derived. Close inspection reveals that the highly secret Me 262 program, Project 1065, was a case study in the sometimes laughable, sometimes tragic comedy that surrounds any similar human endeavor.

Project 1065 was characterized by great mistakes which delayed the program and by equally fantastic lucky breaks which spurred it on. There were men of genius who drove themselves night and day to see that the program succeeded, and equally well motivated leaders whose decisions were nearly catastrophic. From this contradictory environment a truly great airplane emerged.

Buttressing and giving truth to the flashing beauty of the Me 262, which has fascinated artists and modelers over the years, were its remarkable jet engines. It was those Junkers Jumo 004 engines alone which made the *Schwalbe* such a powerful harbinger of the future. German engineers, mostly not from the aviation engine industry, inspired by men like Hans von Ohain, Anselm Franz and Herbert Wagner, worked under impossible conditions to create a jet engine which was qualified for combat.

Despite unbearable shortages of critical materials, despite the lack of test equipment, despite the fact that they were breaking entirely new ground, jet engines were produced in quantity—probably over 6,000 by war's end. Their whistling note of power reverberated throughout the world.

The engines were mated to an airframe which due to a combination of almost spiritual intuition and blind luck was perfect for them. The Me 262's swept wing, wing slats, and heavy armament were put together in a package that was easy to build, maintain and fly. Although 1,443 Me 262's were manufactured during the dying months of World War II, it is estimated that only about 300 actually saw combat.[2] The rest were destroyed in the shrinking Reich which had become an Allied shooting gallery. But these 300, in the hands of some of the most experienced, combat-hardened and dedicated pilots in history, made themselves known to the Allies, and were an object of special concern, even though it was apparent that they could no longer affect the outcome of a battle, much less the war.

2. The best available records from Messerschmitt indicate that 1,443 Me 262s were delivered between March 1944, and April 20, 1945. (Adolf Galland notes that a great number were not completed because of a lack of parts, and that many were destroyed on the ground.)

What then, was the Me 262? It was a fighter of surpassing speed and firepower. It was a reconnaissance plane which could operate with virtual impunity where any other swastika-bearing aircraft would have been shot down. It was, despite all common sense, a bomber which was effectively used by the Germans when they had no other means of penetrating Allied defense. It was a trainer and a night fighter, and the host for a surprising series of radical innovations which ranged from rocket boost to trailed flying gas tanks.

And it was more than this. It was a final challenge from Germany's proud professional aeronautical engineers. It was a thorn in the Allies' side that said, "We may be down but we are not out". It was an inspiration to combat weary pilots who had gone from heady air supremacy to being hounded like vagrants from one primitive airfield to another. These men, who understood perhaps better than any others the travesty of Nazi politics and the hopelessness of the war situation, were able to fly with pride and passion once more. Units which had melted time and again in the heat of the war were finally melded into stout Me 262 formations which carried on to the very end.

The Me 262 was both a fascination and a terror to the Allied pilots who enjoyed

A Schwalbe believed to belong to Kommando Nowotony. a service test unit led by the famous Austrian ace Major Walter Nowotony. The nose gear was notoriously weak; 34% of all Me 262 accidents stemmed from undercarriage problems. (Courtesy Messerschmitt Archiv)

Me 262 production was maintained under the most primitive conditions. Here a forest serves as camouflage for a final assembly line. The German system of contracting sub assemblies to widely separated factories was successful until late in the war when the truck and rail transportation became impossible due to the fuel shortage and strafing Allied fighter bombers. (U.S. Air Force)

their virtual rule over the German skies, and for whom air combat was almost always conducted on their own terms. The Me 262, with its breathtaking performance, would make great curving attacks through the bomber formations, loosing its four powerful 30 mm cannons or the even more remarkable R4M rockets, and then sweep away. To find one in a vulnerable situation, perhaps landing or taking off, brought joy to an Allied fighter pilot's heart.

But most of all, the Me 262 was the product of the men who put their souls in designing aircraft, and the men who maintained and flew them. Born to an unfeeling, uncaring, shortsighted government, nursed to maturity through seemingly endless engine development programs which caused the size and shape of the airframe to change drastically, and finally produced at a time when labor, materials, tools, and fuel were all in short supply, the *Schwalbe* nonetheless emerged as an all-time classic design, the premier fighter plane of WW II, testimony to the intelligence and resilience of the German people, who despite their grievous wounds and malevolent political system were still able to create a masterpiece. Entirely independent of the insignia it bore, or of the crumbling lost cause in whose defense it was deployed, the Me 262 was a patriotic expression of the best in German engineering and courage.

CHAPTER 2

Development Background

The Fokker D. VII was advanced in its method of construction for World War I as the Me 262 was advanced for its method of propulsion in World War II. The thick semi-cantilever wings and steel tube fuselage of the Fokker set the pattern for the next decade, just as the jet engines of Me 262 did.

Almost none of the Me 262 story—its inception, the history of its engines, its employment—is understandable without reviewing briefly the tumultuous expansion of the German Luftwaffe, its incredible early successes, and its growing weakness as its limited strength was spread over Germany's ever expanding front lines.

The Luftwaffe's development process itself is inextricably linked with the painful loss of World War I, the disastrous economic conditions which prevailed in Germany from then until after Hitler's artifical solutions from 1933 on, and the mentality of the German High Command, which was able to update 1918 thinking for 1939 successes, but was unable to go beyond that point in the employment of aircraft.

Germany's proud air effort in the 1914-1918 war laid down a tradition not only of heroism, but also of innovation, material substitution, and incredible production effort. German technology, hampered by the blockade, and initially short of manpower and machines, nonetheless built over 48,000 airplanes in the course of the war, and had in 1918 a creditable array of highly efficient aircraft. Of these the Fokker D.VII and D.VIII are particularly interesting. Like the Me 262 of one war later, they pointed the way to the future. In the case of the Fokker products it was not the engine but the airframe that was advanced. The gas-welded steel-tube fuselage and thick, cantilever wing construction of the two aircraft, unmarred by dozens of flying wires, clearly set the pattern for the next decade's aircraft. By contrast, both the Spad XIII and the Sopwith Snipe, comparable as their performance may have been, represented the end of the World War I development line, with its wire braced, thin section wings, and built-up wood fuselages.

The Germans had forged ahead in the construction of all metal aircraft, too, and the employment of the clumsy but rugged Junkers J-1 trench strafers and the few Junker fighter planes would have been followed by even more aircraft, possibly including a bomber version of the truly advanced Staaken E. 4/20 which appeared briefly after the war as a four engine transport capable of a 140 mph speed.

The Treaty of Versailles stripped Germany of its aircraft building capability just as it stripped it of an air force, and there was a long interregnum in which planes were built surreptitiously, just as pilots were trained under the cloak of civil operations.

Even though these clandestine efforts maintained a thread of military continuity, particularly the oft discussed Russo-German cooperation at Lipetsk, the fact was that there was no tradition being maintained, no progress through the ranks for the hundreds of young company grade officers who had distinguished themselves in combat, and worst of all, no body of air doctrine.

The manufacturers suffered in a similar manner; efforts were concentrated on non-military types, limited in horsepower, and completely conventional in construction. This had the effect of blunting the scope of aviation development in Germany, particularly in engines, where development times were far longer and more expensive than for airframes.

By contrast, in every other major power—England, France, the U.S.A., Russia, Japan, Italy—both military aviation and the manufacture of aircraft and engines continued, even if on a reduced scale. In some cases, the development as well as the progress was slow, because of limited budgets and lack of Congressional or Parliamentary interest. Nevertheless the hard core remained—bright young men still left West Point, Sandhurst, or St. Cyr to join their native air service, and it was these young men who would become the Wing Commanders, Generals, and Air Marshals of the Second World War. Doctrine, though in some cases primitive, and often even erroneous, was maintained, argued about and developed; there was experience in various levels of command available; officers could be rotated between air and staff jobs.

In many respects the relatively small size of the services had a beneficial effect. They were still an elite, even if equipment in almost every air force in the world, with the exception for many years of the French, was largely obsolete and often times even unsafe. And as an elite, they were competitive, and young officers, men like Eaker, Spaatz, and Doolittle, or Sholto Douglas, Leigh Mallory and Park, became identified as having great potential, with the capability to be promoted swiftly to positions of power and influence when the inevitable expansion came.

This did not happen in Germany. The *Reichswehr,* even though it evaded the 100,000 man limitation imposed by Versailles by a number of means, including shorter service periods, was unable to maintain the heritage of the Air Force. In 1935 Hitler officially announced the existence of the *Luftwaffe.* In the initial years of the rearmament the lack of continuity was not too much of a handicap. Retreads from World War I, pilots from the various clandestine training programs and new volunteers were adequate to man what was essentially a training command. There were bomber and fighter units flying obsolescent aircraft like the Heinkel He 51, Arado Ar 68, Junkers Ju 52/3m, and so on, but only the propagandists considered these to be effective weapons.

Hitler's later meteoric string of political successes, dependent as they were upon the threat of a city-razing Air Force, forced the helter skelter expansion of the

The Heinkel He 51 did not differ appreciably from the Fokker D-VII format. It was the first standard fighter of the new Luftwaffe.

Luftwaffe, just as it did of the Army. There was no shortage of volunteers to fill the pilot ranks, and there was even no real shortage of modern aircraft, as the first aircraft programs began to deliver machines like the Messerschmitt Bf 109, Heinkel He 111, Junkers Ju 87 and so on. However, the fabric of leadership was being stretched already; there was a dearth of intermediate commanders, men who could not only fly with a fighter squadron, but supervise its training, make sure its maintenance was up to standard and instill the necessary discipline.

The *Luftwaffe's* participation in the Spanish Civil War proved to be a mixed blessing. On the one hand the test of men and equipment was invaluable, and much was learned about close air support in cooperation with the Army. On the other hand, the success of the Condor Legion sold the Germans on the idea that their lightly armed medium bombers could penetrate a defended target. Perhaps more

OPPOSITE PAGE:

The Messerschmitt Bf 109 was Germany's standard fighter throughout World War II. Over 33,000 were built, more than any other plane except the Russian IL-2 Sturmovik. At the beginning of the war the Bf 109 was equal to any fighter in the world. By 1943, it had fallen behind world standards, and by late 1944 was severely outclassed.

Colonel Werner Moelders, right, (115 victories) was killed in the crash of a Heinkel He 111 in connection with Ernst Udet's funeral. Lieutenant Colonel (later Generalleutnant) Adolf Galland (104 victories) survived the war and enjoyed a prosperous postwar career in aviation. (Luftwaffe Photo)

importantly, it weaned all support away from the concept of a heavy strategic bomber.

Similarly, successes in Poland and then in the West had a dual effect. They provided excellent training, "blooding" commanders and pilots, and giving the best possible experience for combat aviators. Offsetting this there was attrition, and from the very beginning, German losses in the middle leadership were difficult to replace.

The story changed somewhat for the worse with the Battle of Britain. A defeat, although not acknowledged as such at first, it cost bitterly in terms of planes and personnel, and it introduced a new feature into the command element. Goering insisted that his senior staff personnel come from the ranks of the flyers. As a result, men like Adolf Galland and Werner Moelders were quickly brought to the forefront.

Behind them, men of gallantry and bravery, but of less distinction as leaders, were interwoven into the *Luftwaffe* chain of command. It was a fragile linkage, less adaptable, and far less capable than the equivalent in either the R.A.F. or the U.S. Army Air Force.

In an exactly similar way, the German aviation industry had been jerked from its infancy. Where it had been building small numbers of conventional aircraft like the Junkers W-34, and the Focke Wulf Fw 44B *"Stieglitz"*, as well as a handful of advanced types like the Heinkel He 70a *"Blitz"*, it now was engaged in full scale production of modern weapons like the Dornier Do 17 and Junkers Ju 88.

The entire explosion, from official infancy to the strike on Poland took only four years. And this initial leap from the restrictions of Versailles to warfare was climaxed by a virtual freeze on development of new types. The incredible, almost inexplicable first successes of the Luftwaffe in Poland and in France confirmed the German High Command's belief the war could be won with this first generation of combat planes.

Reality soon came, and it was shattering. The air initiative passed over to England on the Western Front, and even after titanic success in Russia, where the opening days of the war were a virtual shooting party for the German pilots, the *Luftwaffe* became spread too thin to be effective. And as it spread, Russia began to recoup its strength from its dispersed aircraft factories and from Lend Lease.

In brief, the *Luftwaffe,* which had sprung almost overnight from clandestine existence into a effective tactical addition to Germany's armies, found itself overextended, locked into aircraft types which were fast becoming obsolete, and handicapped by a shortage of middle level commanders. In addition it had never adopted any sort of rational strategic bombing policy, foregoing the development of aircraft which would have made it possible.

The industry which supported the *Luftwaffe* felt the bite of shortages before others did, for in Hitler's thinking, aircraft were subordinate to tanks and to submarines, and the factories of Europe that he controlled puttered along at little more than their pre-war production rates, barely able to fill vacancies caused by combat attrition.

It is against this background that the Messerschmitt Me 262 must be considered, for it highlights the almost non-professional mileu in which it was born, and gives some insight into the blindness of the German leaders which first delayed its development and then misdirected its employment.

Oddly enough, the Messerschmitt Me 262's genesis can be attributed to an arch-competitor of Willy Messerschmitt, whose rugged individualism will be investigated later. The competitor was Ernst Heinkel, a controversial man whose love-hate relationship with the German Air Ministry would continue to the last days of the war. He wanted to develop fast aircraft for sale to the military, and he also wanted to develop an engine-building capability similar to the one enjoyed by the Junkers *Flugzeug* and *Motorenwerke A.G.* He wished, if possible, to fly Heinkel aircraft with Heinkel engines, and to be able to arm the resurgent *Luftwaffe* and any other buyer with this combined product.

Ernst Heinkel was a controversial manufacturer of high quality, high performance aircraft. From left, Erich Warsitz, Heinkel, Dr. von Ohain.

As indicated before, the entire German engine industry had been crippled by the restrictions of the Treaty of Versailles, and by the economic problems which had been worse in Germany than in most places in the world. It had attempted to make up for lost time by building license versions of aircraft engines from other countries, and by buying, for study, copies of the leading engines in the world. Nonetheless, despite the efforts of engineers at Daimler Benz, Junkers and B.M.W., Germany was not yet making an inline engine of Rolls Royce merit, nor a radial comparable to U.S. Pratt & Whitney or Wright standards. A new invention would change all this.

CHAPTER 3

𝕵et 𝕰ngine 𝕯evelopment

The Heinkel He S 3b engine, which powered the Heinkel He 178, was an outgrowth of this model engine, made under Dr. von Ohain's direction by master machinist Max Hahn, shown here in Bartels & Becker's repair shop. The total cost was slightly more than 1,000 marks.

einkel did not have experience in engine building, nor did he have the engineers, tools, or financial capability to begin to compete in conventional piston engine manufacture. Thus when his friend, R. W. Pohl of the University of Goettingen recommended to him a student of his, Hans von Ohain, Heinkel was more than interested. Von Ohain, a student of applied physics and aerodynamics, had already obtained patents on a turbojet engine using a centrifugal compressor.

The concept of the jet engine was not new, for the idea of propulsion by reaction went back at least to the steam powered Aeliopile and was highlighted in engineering literature in applications as industrial gas turbines as early as 1906. A very close relative, the turbo supercharger, received intensive development coincidentally from 1906 on. Auguste Rateau of France applied a turbo supercharger to an aircraft engine in 1916, and was followed in the United States by Dr. Sanford Moss' very successful experiments with General Electric turbo superchargers on the Liberty engine. The problems of control and the inability of the turbine wheel to withstand the tremendous temperatures of the exhaust gases were difficult to overcome, but patient experimentation led to the successful units operated on many U.S. aircraft in World War II.

Jet engines, as possible powerplants for aircraft, were alluded to in the 1920s, and a primitive piston engine driven type had been built by France's Professor Coanda as long ago as 1910. A. A. Griffith of the Royal Aircraft Establishment was an early proponent of the concept, advocating that a compressor of high enough efficiency could be built to create what would be today called a turbo-prop engine. A change of assignments and the general economies resulting from the world wide depression in 1931 kept Griffith from proceeding with his ideas.

Flying Officer Frank Whittle went a step further than Griffith, proposing a somewhat simpler engine which would not have a propeller, but instead would apply its power purely as exhaust. He persisted, and after years of study, effort and frustration, turned to private industry to create a working jet engine, the WU, in April, 1937. Two more years of privately financed experimentation was necessary before the British Air Ministry was convinced in 1939 that the jet engine was practical, and Whittle's W-1 engine was flown in the Gloster E 28/39 on May 15, 1941.

But this was all in the future, and von Ohain was entirely unaware of Whittle's efforts at the time. His own engine differed in all details from Whittle's and is another illustration of how men of genius, in different parts of the world, can labor under entirely different conditions to provide equal but alternate solutions to the same problems.

(It is fascinating to listen to von Ohain recount these pioneering years today; he depreciates his own role in the process, and praises all of his coworkers. He is a bluff, hearty, jolly man, looking 20 younger than his age, and fascinated not half so much by the past as by the future.)

Heinkel was particularly attracted to von Ohain's concepts for a number of reasons. First, the sole *raison-d'etre* of the jet engine was speed, and Heinkel was inordinately fascinated with fast airplanes. Second, it seemed to offer Heinkel a way within his means into the engine industry. The jet engine was built largely of sheet metal, with which Heinkel's workers were familiar, and any complex parts could be subcontracted to any one of a dozen factories in Germany.

To von Ohain, it must have seemed like a dream come true. This young student, just out of college, was suddenly able to apply the resources of one of his country's most advanced aircraft plants to his pet dream—the jet engine.

A test engine was begun in April 1936; it was completed and run in March 1937, at a total expenditure of a little less than $20,000.00.

The HeS-3b produced only 1,100 pounds of thrust, but this was sufficient for the tiny, experimental He 178.

On August 27, 1939, Flugkapitan Erich Warsitz made the world's first jet flight from a field at Marienehe, Germany. The impact of that flight on world aviation economics and society is still being felt.

The test engine was a success, and it convinced Heinkel to proceed with the almost buccaneer-like confidence that he showed on a dozen projects during the war. Heinkel was not always too successful in his dealings with the Air Ministry but he was always daring, and many of his most brilliant projects—the Heinkel He 100 fighter, the superfast Heinkel He 119 reconnaissance plane, the He 280 jet fighter, and the magnificent He 219 night fighter were all built with little encouragement and sometimes with downright opposition. Heinkel immediately began the construction of an airframe, the Heinkel He 178, and called upon von Ohain to create a flightworthy engine of about 1,800 pounds of thrust. His demands were optimistic, but the He S-3b which resulted did achieve about 1,110 pounds of thrust for a weight of 795 pounds. It would be enough to make history.

The airframe, designed by a talented team composed of Dipl. Ing. Heinrich Hertel, Karl Schwaerzler and the gifted twin brothers Siegfried and Walter Guenter, was the simplest, smallest imaginable. A tiny, 23 foot 3½ inch span shoulder wing surmounted a simple tubular 24 foot 6 inch long fuselage; long curved ducting brought inlet air into the radical new engine, and the exhaust followed a relatively long tail pipe.

Flugkapitän Erich Warsitz, who had earlier distinguished himself by flying the almost equally revolutionary rocket powered Heinkel He 176 at Peenemunde, became very involved in the project, and on August 27, 1939, lifted the little aircraft off the Heinkel airfield at Marienehe. It was the first flight under jet power in the world, and neither von Ohain, Heinkel or Warsitz could have conceived that 40 years later their invention would be the very cornerstone of many of the world's achievements—and problems.

Von Ohain's achievement was in no way diminished by the close competition of Whittle, nor of the other inventors in the field in Germany, Hungary, Russia, France and Sweden. His was the first jet to fly, and it was his efforts which convinced the German Air Ministry to begin supporting the reaction engine in earnest. There

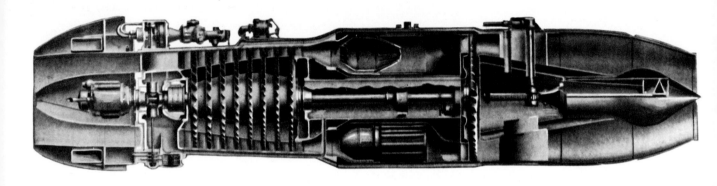

Dr. Anselm Franz designed the Junkers Jumo 004 engine which powered the Messerschmitt Me 262. Although deliberately a conservative design, and "frozen" for production far too early in its development, the axial flow 004 was very successful. More than 6,000 were built before the end of World War II. (Photo Courtesy Dr. Anselm Franz)

had been small investments in Paul Schmidt's pulse jet invention as early as 1931, and during the mid 1930s further money had been alloted to rockets as anti-aircraft weapons and as aircraft propulsion systems. Hans A. Mauch headed rocket development in the Air Ministry, and began to back the development of both jet engines and suitable airframes.

With his backing a whole series of jet programs was undertaken, including Walther ramjets, Schmidt pulsejets (the type used to power the V-1), the Heinkel/von Ohain engine, the turbine engines of Herbert Wagner at Junkers, and a pair of programs at BMW/Bramo, one of which derived from the pioneering 1928 work of Dr. Herman Oesterich.

Apparently feeling that Heinkel was already committed to the program, the German Air Ministry in 1938 solicited Robert Lusser, chief of development of Messerschmitt to investigate the possibility of an aircraft using the new power plants, one which would have a speed capability of 850 km/h and a one hour endurance—this at a time when front line fighters were barely cracking the 500 km/h mark. (Lusser, ironically, would leave Messerschmitt and join Heinkel, where he designed the rival—and losing—Heinkel He 280 fighter.) At Messerschmitt, the challenge was accepted by a team headed by Woldemar Voigt, whose progress we will detail in the next chapter.

The airframe design was predicated on the receipt, by December 1939, of flightworthy engines from BMW capable of developing slightly more than 1,300 pounds of thrust. Fortunately for the program, other development lines were being undertaken at Junkers.

The original engine being developed at Junkers under Herbert Wagner's direction was not progressing well, and in the fall of 1939 a 39-year old graduate of the University of Graz, Dr. Anselm Franz, began work on the engine which became the Junkers Jumo 004, the engine which would power the Me 262.

The 004 was to set a number of firsts. It was the first successful axial flow engine, a type which has subsequently become the standard in jet engine design. It was also the first jet engine to go into volume production, the first to enter combat, and the first to be capable of using an afterburner.

Franz embarked on the program with the vision and precision which characterizes him even today. He determined from the start not to try to wring the most performance from his engine, but instead set conservative, achievable goals. He really intended the first engine to serve as a baseline upon which more advanced engines could be built. In the event, the requirement for the Jumo 004 was so great that its design was "frozen" early in its career, and it was pressed into production long before Franz considered it fully ready.

An experimental engine, the 004A was first run on October 11, 1940, and by January, 1941, had developed almost 1,000 pounds of thrust. Some redesign was called for, and by December, 1941, more than 2,200 pounds of thrust were being demonstrated on the test stands, an incredible increase, and one that put all rival jet engines into the shade.

The engine was flight tested beneath a Messerschmitt Bf 110 on March 15, 1942. On July 18, 1942, two of the preproduction engines were used on the first flight of the Me 262.

The 004A engine was not suitable for production because of a variety of reasons, including its excessive use of strategic materials, and its weight to power ratio. The first production engine, the 004B-1, was delivered in June, 1943, and a flight was made with these engines in a Messerschmitt Me 262 in October. An optimistic time-between-overhaul period of 50 hours was approved, an objective that was never reached.

The complexities of developing a jet engine were sometimes overcome in almost simplistic ways; when the 004B-1 began to have vibration failures in the turbine buckets, a professional musician was hired. With his perfect pitch, he could determine the natural frequencies of individual blades in an assembled turbine wheel by means of a violin bow. His gentle bowing led to the solution of the vibration problem by tapering the blades slightly to increase their natural frequency, and by reducing the operating RPM of the engine from 9,000 to 8,700 RPM.

Let us now turn to the development of the Messerschmitt Me 262 itself, which went on concurrently with the efforts of Franz's team. The further development of the engines will be discussed in the context of the aircraft as a whole.

Birth of the Me 262

The tentative interest of the *Reichsluftfahrtministerium* (RLM) in jet aircraft extended to seeking a proposal from Messerschmitt for a twin-engine fighter which would use the axial flow turbojets being developed by BMW. The proposal was tendered to a company that, despite all propaganda before and during the war, and despite the controversy that swirled around Willy Messerschmitt, was run on lines which would make modern behavioral psychologists smile benignly.

Deep in totalitarian Germany, there existed a company democratically managed, a company that, in fact, allowed its advanced design teams to function on a committee basis. Woldemar Voigt has said that in America management by committee has a sour note, but in the amazingly beneficient climate of the Messerschmitt team, it worked and worked well. At Messerschmitt the committee leader was ultimately responsible for any decision and for its timeliness.[1]

Voigt, who had joined Messerschmitt in 1933 and became head of the Project Bureau in 1939, attributes the unusual successes of the Messerschmitt team to a spirit fostered by Willy Messerschmitt himself.

Messerschmitt was born in Frankfurt am Main on June 26, 1898, into very comfortable circumstances. He got into aviation early, and enjoyed a fascinating, profitable 56 year career before his death on September 15, 1978. Never very popular at the highest levels within the Third Reich, his undoubted engineering capability and his talent as a manufacturer made him indispensable. Messerschmitt ran the company to please himself as an engineer, and he ran it in a way in which most engineers like to work.

Messerschmitt, ironically, was not a "people person"; rather he concentrated on the whole technical picture of a program. He was very sparing of praise. Voigt recalls that just after the successful first flight of the Me 262, everyone was elated as they walked back from the flight line. Messerschmitt paid Voigt his highest

1. From a talk delivered to the American Aviation Historical Society at the National Air and Space Museum by Woldemar Voigt, May, 1974.

compliment, saying, "You know, Herr Voigt, you might have become a good detail designer".

There were two basic engineering groups in the total of about 175 engineers in place at Messerschmitt's Augsburg factory at the beginning of the war. Of these, about 30% were in advanced design, and about 70% in hardware, structural design and so on. Voigt says that two entirely different breeds of engineers were involved, and Messerschmitt evolved a very simple and basic mechanism to obtain the best from both teams and from the system.

For the advanced design team, there was simply no budget. Money was not something to be considered; if something needed to be done, whatever money spent to do it was deemed well spent. On the other hand, manhours were extremely limited, especially the manhours available to toolmakers. Voigt says that lack of tooling capacity was one of the basic recurring weaknesses of the German air industry, one that was never properly addressed. As a result, while no thought was given to the expense of an engineering solution, much thought was given to the manhours involved.

The advanced design team was given a series of tasks by Messerschmitt. It was supposed to survey the field and see what was possible within the state of the art, and where the state of the art could be stretched; to develop a concept and sell it to the Air Ministry, and then do the essential aerodynamics and configuration engineering. Its responsibility ended with the acceptance of a fully developed mock-up and a signed contract for development. The "hardware" engineers then took over.

On the other hand, and never far from the thinking of the advance design group, was the pay plan Messerschmitt used to keep everyone on the same team. He rewarded Voigt with bonuses, and Voigt in turn had the perogative to give his engineers raises. In part the amount of increase was predicated upon the design entering volume production. So it was in their interest to achieve advanced designs while still paying strong attention to production considerations.

The two sets of engineering teams worked well under Messerschmitt's "committee system" simply because it was a part of Messerschmitt philosophy *not* to put too much emphasis on who was "boss". Instead, the specialists on the teams were given a charter to reach consensus on problems. Each team member felt a responsibility for the key decisions deriving from these committee agreements, and each saw his own speciality in the context of the entire department, or of the company. During all of this interactive process, Messerschmitt worked intimately with each specialist. (Voigt says that up until 1943, Messerschmitt personally reviewed each drawing, and made changes on most.)

Normally, a loose committee arrangement in a high pressure aircraft development organization might be a formula for disaster. The Messerschmitt system of assuming that the specialists on the line knew more about the problem than the boss, and that the boss knew more about the problem than Voigt, and that Voigt knew more about the problem than Messerschmitt, worked well. Voigt's administrative assistant once made an informal study that revealed that only three times in five years were there instances when consensus was not reached, and Voigt had to make an overruling decision.

The material that Voigt and his team had to work from, on the Me 262 project, was scanty indeed. They had a reasonable idea of the weight and power of the prospective jet engines, and they knew that an endurance of one hour and a speed of 850 km/h was the desired design goal. Rudolph Seitz became primarily responsible for the design with Dipl. Ing. Hornung laying out the draft design sketches.

A number of single and twin-engine configurations were toyed with, including some similar to those used on other fighters at a later date, as in the case of the de Havilland Vampire, with its central nacelle and twin tail booms, or the pod and boom configuration used on the Messerschmitt P 1101, the Bell X-5 and many others. Single-engine solutions had a number of drawbacks in terms of performance, however, and the first definitive designs were twin-engined.

Without any previous experience with jets, the team felt the most obvious course was to mount them on the wings as piston planes did, running the engines through the main spar in a manner similar to that used on the English Electric *Canberra* of about ten years later. The initial aircraft design, while clean, was conventional, using a straight wing and a tail wheel undercarriage. The final version of the aircraft would have the wing swept, a tricycle type landing gear, and minor variations in the canopy, empennage and so on. The amazing fact is that the basic configuration was derived by "committee consensus", with minimal wind tunnel tests being run. Voigt remembers that the only transonic wind tunnel in Germany was so small that only a 7/8 inch model of the Me 262 could be tested, and the data to be obtained simply would not be valid. He does not recall today why low speed wind tunnel tests were not made, but he regards the successful airframe as a tribute to the reasoning process of his team.

The wing was too thin to stow the landing gear, so a fuselage with a triangular cross section was developed by Ludwig Bölkow. This imparted the characteristic shark-like appearance which the airplane was to retain throughout its career, and which provided an outstanding field of view for the pilot as well.

The engineers discovered that the airplane's extra power from its two engines could not be converted into speed, because of the sharp rise in the drag curve. Voigt's designers used the power to permit an increase in the fuel load, and made room for four 30 mm cannon (and provisions for as many as six). This decision, made early in the game, was ultimately going to be the reason for choosing the Me 262 over the competing Heinkel He 280.

As time passed, a series of changes in engine size and weight created some real problems. The center of gravity of the airplane was too far forward, and the easiest solution was to have the outer panels of the wings swept back, a somewhat crude approach similar to that applied to the Curtiss *Hell Divers* of the 1930's. At the same time, it was realized that the through-the-wing design would limit both engine size

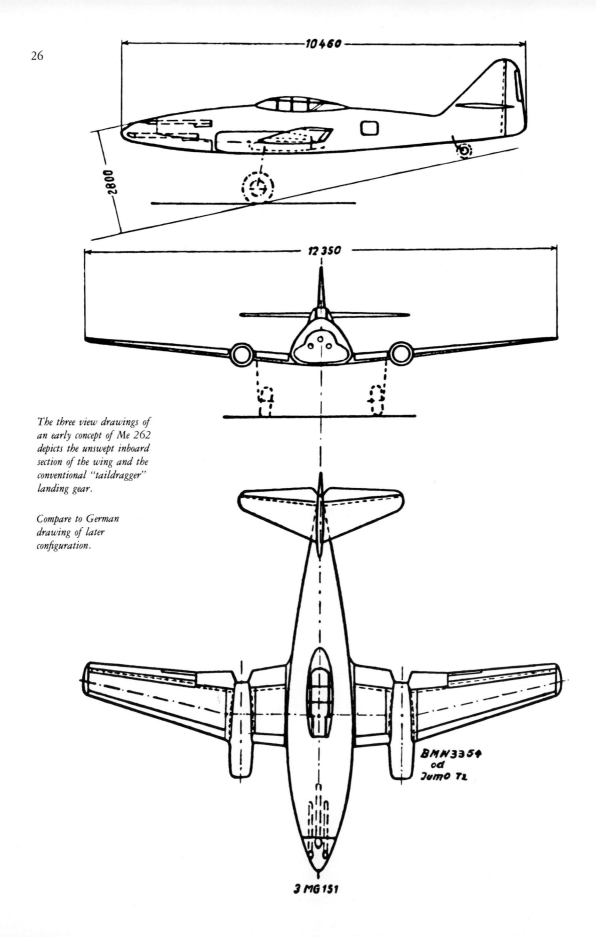

10 460

2800

12 350

The three view drawings of
an early concept of Me 262
depicts the unswept inboard
section of the wing and the
conventional "taildragger"
landing gear.

Compare to German
drawing of later
configuration.

BMW 3354
od
Jumo T2

3 MG 151

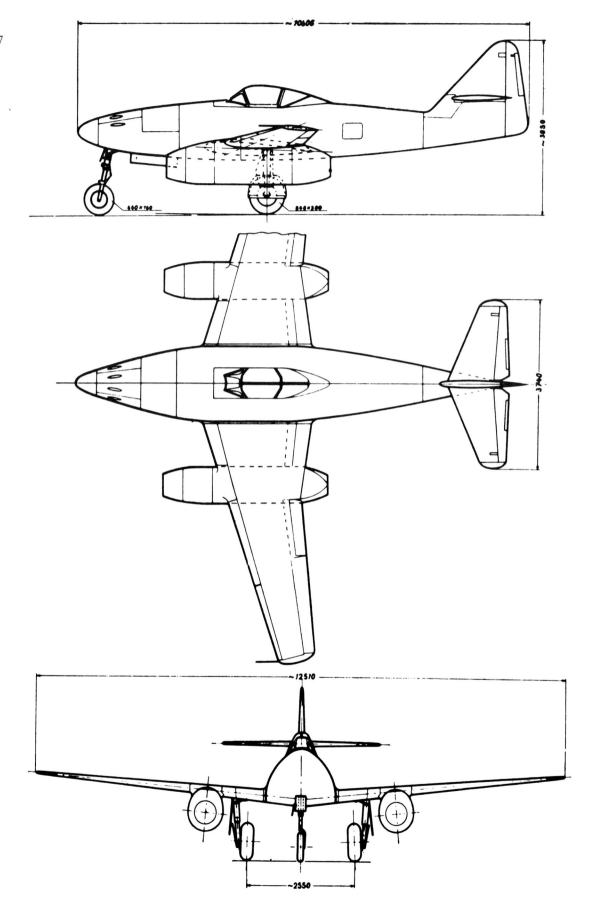

and alternate engine installation. It was decided to place the nacelles under the wing. Both these decisions, fortuitously arrived at, were to pay enormous dividends to the Me 262 and to many succeeding aircraft.

By May 15, 1940, the basic Messerschmitt Me 262 planform was almost complete—there were still some changes coming—and the aircraft was submitted to the RLM. The RLM responded somewhat indifferently, for these were the heady days of July 1940, when Hitler was enjoying the euphoria resulting from his successful blitzkrieg in the West, but three prototypes were ordered. The Me 262 was a back-burner project for the German Air Force, for it seemed entirely possible that the war would be brought to a successful conclusion with the equipment in hand.

A further factor which tended to reduce the urgency of airframe production was the difficulty BMW was having getting the required thrust from the 003 engine. Anselm Franz was busy with the Junkers Jumo 004, but it, too, was having difficulties, and a first flight date could not be stipulated.

Somewhat nonplussed, the Messerschmitt engineers pressed on with the three experimental aircraft, and made an interim decision to fit the number one aircraft, Me 262 V1 (code letters PC+UA) with a Junkers Jumo 210G piston engine of about 750 horsepower. Oddly enough, the Me 262 V1 flew very well on its single piston engine, although it naturally had a long take off run. *Flugkapitan* (an honorary title given civilian test pilots with more than 1,000 hours flying time) Fritz Wendel made the first flight on April 18, 1941, which helped convince the RLM to order five test and 20 pre-production aircraft.

In November 1941, seven months after the first flight, two flight-cleared, BMW 003 turbojets were fitted to the Me 262 V1. Fortunately, the piston engine was retained as a precautionary measure. After a long period of testing, Wendel made a tri-motor take-off on March 26, 1942, which ended in a hair raising single-engine landing when both turbine power plants failed. It was the beginning of an interminable series of delays for the BMW 003 engines, delays which took them right out of the Me 262 program.

The value of having a professional test pilot of Wendel's caliber was amply proved on this flight. (Wendel was a gifted pilot who had set the world's absolute speed record of 469.2 mph in the brutish Me 109R—actually the Me 209V1—on April 26, 1939. It was a record which lasted for 30 years, until Daryl Greenamyer eclipsed it in his specially modified Grumman Bearcat.) The compressor blades of the BMW 003 engines failed, flaming them out one after the other, and Wendel had to jam the throttle of the Jumo 210G engine through the firewall to maintain enough airspeed to keep flying. He made a circle and landed, saving the airplane, and probably the program, for it is doubtful if the RLM would have continued to be interested had the airplane been destroyed.

The Jumo 004 was not only the better bet by now, but the only bet, and Franz's conservative policies were beginning to pay off. The 004 was slightly heavier and

The first of the initial three prototype Me 262 VI (PC + UA) shown here with the Junker Jumo 210 G piston engine in the nose and two BMW 003 jet engines in the underwing nacelles. Note how the vertical surface is shaped differently than on later models. (Messerschmitt Archiv)

larger than the BMW it replaced, and the underslung nacelle had to be increased about 16% in length and 10% in girth. The third prototype, Me 262 V3 (code letter PC + UC) was modified to accept the new engines, and also had its vertical tail surfaces increased to compensate for the additional side area of the larger nacelles.

Wendel was called to duty again to handle the first pure jet powered flights of the Me 262, and after several taxi-trials, attempted, on July 18, 1942, to make the first flight. He aborted his initial attempt, for he found that the tail down attitude of the conventional landing gear rendered the elevators completely ineffective. It was suggested that he make another try, applying brakes momentarily at the 112 mph unstick speed, so that the Me 262 would tip up, put the elevators into the airstream, and make take-off possible. (At least this was the hope of the non-flying engineer who suggested it).

One can only speculate on Wendel's thoughts at about 110 mph as the runway disappeared behind him, but he followed the suggestion and the *Schwalbe* lifted off in pure jet flight. The joy Wendel must have felt as the *Schwalbe* transitioned from an earthbound, underpowered novelty, into a powerful, vibrant new experience is felt again by any pilot making his first flight in a jet. As the wheels retract, clunking

solidly into their faired position, as the flaps are brought up, balancing the desire for a faster airspeed against their structural limitations, as speed builds and noise and vibration fall off, a jet turns from something rather ordinary into an emotional experience. One feels one's power extend into the very wings, for the jet, climbing and accelerating, is a totally different experience for a piston engine trained pilot.

There must have been other thoughts in Wendel's mind, too. A trained test pilot, he was watching his temperatures, his rpms, sensing the feel of the aircraft, keeping the field location in mind in case of an emergency, mentally checking just what he would have to do if an engine failed, and so on. But he must also have felt a certainty that the Messerschmitt Me 262 was a thing apart, a totally new venture in the world of flight.

The first landing was successful, and it was followed in a few hours by another test flight, where once again the intuitive sense of a test pilot was to prove its worth. The Me 262 had been built with sweep only outboard of the engines on the outer wing panels, but Wendel discovered serious airflow difficulties in banking flight; as a result it was decided to make the wing thicker at the inboard section, and also to carry the sweep angle across the thickened section. The leading edge slots, used so well on the Bf 109, now extended all the way across the wing, another forecast for the future. The change resulted in a 30% increase in lift.

The conventional two main and one tail wheel arrangement was a serious disadvantage for the Me 262, for the blast of jet engines not only blew chunks out of hard surface runways, but also rendered the elevators ineffective. This is the Me 262 V2 (PC + UB). (Messerschmitt Archiv)

The open flames which emerged from a jet engine were always disconcerting, and sometimes dangerous. (Air Force Museum)

The chronology of the *Schwalbe's* development in the 34 months from its first pure jet flight to the end of the war is much more meaningful if the key events are related to the larger world of Germany's grinding defeat. If viewed separately, these events are similar to those of any development program: progress, failure, meetings, decisions, change orders, reversed decisions, panic, and so on. When tied to the ever deteriorating war situation, however, several things become manifest. The first, of course, was the growing realization among the Nazi leaders of the Me 262's potential, a realization that grew from hope to faith to delusion. Second, one finds that many of the program decisions were correct, given the circumstances, and that some of the more notorious mistakes did not really have an effect. Finally, it is easy to see that the success of the program was almost irrelevant, for by the time the aircraft could have been employed effectively, Germany was moribund, ringed on all sides by powerful enemies who were better fed, better equipped, better led and extraordinarily motivated. Germany's own substance, never on a par with its foes, was already consumed in the fire of five years of warfare, and its very life's blood, its young soldiers, had been squandered in battles that now had little meaning.

When Wendel made that July 18th flight, however, the German armies had apparently recovered from the dismal first Russian winter, and were triumphantly driving towards the Caucasus. Aircraft production, while increasing, had not really gotten into its stride, and though the recent May 30-31, 1,000 plane British raid on Cologne had been sobering and boded ill for the future, other fronts were quite promising. Rommel had just missed his march to Alexandria, and had settled into positions at El Alamein; in less than a month, the British and Canadians would receive what the Germans perceived as a bloody nose at Dieppe. In short, the first flight occurred at a time when Germany, although terribly overextended, was still powerful.

In August, it was decided to build five additional prototypes and twice that many pre-production aircraft. As in any modern test program, individual test aircraft were identified to pursue specific test areas—armament installations, communication variants, and so on. It was agreed that the pre-production aircraft would be fitted with tricycle gear, which would overcome the elevator blanketing problem as well as the detrimental effect the jet blast had on asphalt and concrete runways.

By December, 1942, however, the disaster at Stalingrad was shaping up, one that could be seen dimly even through the clouded official communiques, and with terrifying clarity at German headquarters. It was decided by the RLM to begin production of the Me 262 at a rate of 20 per month beginning in January 1944, allowing one year for the simultaneous development of the still teething Junkers Jumo 004 engine and the new and promising Me 262 airframe.

Testing continued, and on May 22, 1943, *Generalleutnant* Adolf Galland came to Lechfield to fly the aircraft. Although the American 8th Air Force was still building, pecking at the western areas of Germany and concentrating its training effort on occupied France, the British air offensive under "Bomber" Harris was

Although tricycle landing gear were becoming increasingly popular in the west, German designers had preferred the "conventional" arrangement because they were lighter, easier to service and more suitable for rough field conditions. The fifth prototype (Me 262 V-5, PC + UE) was fitted with a fixed tricycle gear for test purposes. (Messerschmitt Archiv)

reaching full stride, and, though Galland could not know it, the horror of Hamburg was but one month away. Galland was more than aware, however, of the relative trends in air strength; he knew that the Allies were building up at an alarming rate, even while Germany's strength was declining. His immediate reaction to the Me 262 was one of both excitement and relief—excitement at flying a clearly superior weapon which opened entirely new tactical possibilities, and relief at the prospect that Germany, which he knew could never again achieve quantitative superiority for its fighters against its enemies, might gain a significant qualitative superiority.[2]

Galland's enthusiasm caused the Me 262 to be released for production on June 2, 1943, a time when the Germans had already been driven out of North Africa, and when the Italian island Pantelleria surrendered to Allied air bombardment, clearing the way for the invasion of Sicily. Despite the clear ebbing of German fortunes in all theaters, the decision to mass produce the Me 262 was squelched for almost three months, and when in August *General* Erhard Milch boosted fighter production goals to a projected 4,000 per month, the Me 262 was virtually ignored.

This vacillation was not confined to aircraft production programs; Hitler had just gone through a similar period of hesitation before launching the catastrophic "Operation Citadel" at Kursk in July. Nor were the difficulties solely political, for the great fundamental weakness of the German air weapon was the paucity of

2. Letter from General Galland, dated 6 December 1978.

Another view of Me 262 V5, showing the Borsig rocket installation for assisted takeoff. (Messerschmitt Archiv)

machine tools.[3] The necessary equipment to expand Me 262 production was not available, except at the expense of the production of existing types, which were being consumed at a fearful rate.

Amid the agony of these defeats in battle and defeats at the conference table, the Me 262 program pursued its own life, following an amazingly normal path of development, equipment tests, modification and innovation. Testing was much inhibited by the lack of prototypes; even in November 1943, when the question of carrying bombs first became a crisis, there was only one prototype Me 262, the V3, available for testing. The Me262 V1, V2 and V4 had all been destroyed, while the V5 was damaged.

As a result, some of the equipment intended for production aircraft was tested on other airplanes. The Me 309 V3, a competitor with the Focke Wulf Ta 152, was

3. Report of Technical Intelligence Survey, prepared by Brigadier General George M. McDonald, Director of Intelligence, U.S. Strategic Air Force in Europe, 31 July 1945.

The final gear installation was clean and efficient, although both retraction and extension times were slow. This is the first preproduction aircraft Me 262 V6, in which the new fully retractable gear was installed.

used to assist in development of the pressure cabin and the ejection seat intended for the Me 262 production versions. Similarly, the Bf 109 V-23 was used to test the proposed tricycle gear arrangement.

The fifth prototype, the Me 262 V5, was fitted with a fixed nosegear arrangement, and also with Borsig rockets to assist its takeoff.

At about the same time, the first pre-production aircraft Me 262 V6 (Code VI + AA) joined the test programs. It was very close in appearance to the production versions, for it had a fully retractable tricycle gear, cleaned-up nacelles and a slightly revised empennage. Me 262 V7 (code letter VI + AB) joined it shortly, and although similar to its predecessor, was fitted with a primitive pressure cabin.

The Me 262 was demonstrated to Hitler on November 26, 1943, and although he often had an immediate affinity for the unusual, he was clearly not overwhelmed by the aircraft. Obsessed as always with the idea of the offensive, and with reprisal, he saw the aircraft as a means to evade the pervasive Allied fighter screen that had rendered his once mighty bomber fleet virtually impotent. He knew that the invasion was a certainty within the next few months, and hoped that the Me 262 could serve as a fighter bomber to drive the Allies off the beaches.

Albert Speer who had been Minister for Armament for less than a year, but had already made enormous strides towards bringing Germany to its full armament potential, gave the Me 262 top priority.[4] If Hitler had felt differently, the light metals and other scarce commodities directed to the *Schwalbe* program would have

4. In *Inside the Third Reich* by Albert Speer (New York, The MacMillan Company, 1970). Speer indicated that both he and Milch attempted to subvert Hitler's order as much as possible to continue production of the Me 262 as a fighter.

inevitably been consumed by other components of the production program. Thus, six months before the notorious *Führer-befehl* of June 8, 1944, which limited the Messerschmitt Me 262 to the bomber role, Hitler had provided the impetus to really get the program rolling.[5] And this trade-off, the plus of the priority against the minus of the bomber designation, is symbolic of the politics of the entire jet effort.

The key element in the late deployment of the Me 262 was the protracted development period of the jet engines. Despite Franz's deliberately conservative approach, there were too many factors working against a blitz engine program. First of all there was no background of experience to draw on; Junkers and every other jet engine manufacturing company were plowing new ground. Strategic materials were very limited, and production engines had to be made largely of sheet metal parts, protected from oxidation by an aluminum coating, and designed so that air cooling could keep the temperature of the sheet metal within acceptable limits.

Franz had started with just a few key people, and as he was unable, under the Reich's labor priority system, to hire engineers from the already hard pressed piston engine community, he was forced to take new engineers, just graduated from school, and press them into service. It was not until 1944 that the entire jet division grew to more than 500 people.[6]

Test equipment was similarly in short supply. At start up, there were no special stands which could test turbines, compressor, and combustors independently, under controlled conditions. Entire engines had to be built up and run for tests, and it was sometimes difficult to isolate a problem in one part of the engine, or to keep it from propagating one problem into another.[7]

Despite these problems, and despite the fact that it was hardly fully developed, the Junkers Jumo 004B-1 was "frozen" for production in June, 1944, the month that the Allies invaded France, and the Russians prepared for their gigantic offensive which would carry them to Berlin and beyond.

Unsatisfactory as the "frozen" Jumo may have been, production deliveries of the engine began to build rapidly, and with it acceptance of the Me 262 by the Luftwaffe. Twenty-eight were delivered in June, 59 in July, 20 in August, 91 in September, and 117 in October. This was at a time when U.S. aircraft production was moving towards 100,000 aircraft per year, when the front collapsed in France, when Bulgaria

---

5. In attachment two of a letter from Ludwig Bolkow to Brigadefuhrer von Schultz-Tratzig, October 25, 1944, there is some indication that enthusiastic subordinates overzealously interpreted Hitler's directive about the use of the Me 262 as a bomber, and that Hitler himself recognized its worth as a fighter.

6. Anselm Franz very modestly discusses his contribution in an article "The Development of the Jumo 004 Engine" in the book *The Jet Age,* edited by Walter J. Boyne and Donald S. Lopez, The Smithsonian Press, 1979.

7. Ibid.

was occupied, when Rumania switched sides, and when the Russians swept to the borders of Hungary.

In an almost touching manner, the professionals at Messerschmitt and elsewhere continued to develop the aircraft, meanwhile trying to get Hitler's "bomber" order revoked. They succeeded in November.

Eager *Luftwaffe* pilots had since June 1944 been training in the first production version, the Me 262A-1a. *Erprobungskommando* 262 was the unit at Lechfield which endeavored both to transition fighter pilots to the revolutionary new aircraft and to develop suitable tactics for its use. The unit was formed in December 1943 and began operations as early as April, 1944, with the acquisition of 15 pre-production fighters. As might be expected, the maintenance requirements of the temperamental engines, combined with the ordinary difficulties encountered with the introduction of any new aircraft, made progress slow but the first kill was scored on July 26, 1944. Oddly enough, despite the vast experience of the Germans in air combat, no suitable doctrine for the employment of the Me 262 was ever developed, and both Steinhoff's and Galland's accounts of their fabled JG 7 and JV 44's efforts late in the war reveal that they were still seeking the correct formula for employment.

The problem was compounded in part, of course, by the effects of Hitler's order to develop the Me 262 as a bomber, for this meant that not only did the aircraft have to be modified for the bombing role, but also that two sets of tactics had to be devised, one for fighters and one for bombers, and that two sets of pilots would have to be trained. On the one hand were the old stagers, the fighter pilots who formed the residual cream of the *Luftwaffe*, a heady combination of veterans who had been fighting since the Spanish Civil War, some of whom had thousands of hours and hundreds of aerial victories, and the relative newcomers, with only a few hundred hours and perhaps only a few victories. On the other hand there was a pool of bomber and even transport pilots, whose aging Heinkel He 111's, Junkers Ju 88's and so on could no longer live in the air, and who had a great deal of experience in instrument and formation flying.

Each mission called for different aircraft, different support equipment, and different tactics; there was simply not enough time left to the 1000-year Reich to develop either program. Conversion training to an aircraft of the Me 262's performance was laughable in its austere simplicity. While the Me 262 was easier to fly than the Me 109 when everything was going well, the temperamental engines, high speed capability and tendency for the lateral controls to stiffen at those high speeds made it deserving of a prolonged, intensive training program.

Actual training seemed to vary from pilot to pilot; Adolf Galland replied "Almost none" when asked how much training he received in the 262. Late in the war when everything had gone to pieces, pilots sometimes received little more than a cockpit checkout before being launched into combat.

In late 1944, however, when the Russian armies were digesting the great gains all along their enormous front, and the Allies had temporarily outrun their supply systems and were moving slowly, in accordance with Eisenhower's plans, across a broad front in France, there was still a semblance of normality within the high priority Me 262 training program. Small groups of experienced fighter and bomber pilots, as well as some "hot shot" cadets, were sent to Lechfield to *III/Ergaenzungs-jagdgeschwader* 2. All had had some time in piston engine fighters under conditions designed to familiarize them with the unusual throttle applications required for the difficult to start and slow to accelerate jets. An intensive short course of ground school instruction on the Me 262 was followed by limited time flying twin engine aircraft, primarily for the benefit of the fighter pilots and students, who would not have had experience in "engine out" techniques. After some experience in starting, and stopping engines, they were given an eight hour flight course. The syllabus[8] was as follows:

FLIGHT	SUBJECT MATTER
1 & 2	Flights around the landing field, making as many landings as possible in the half hour period alloted.
3 & 4	One hour flights at altitude for general handling and limited aerobatics.
5	One flight to 30,000 feet for one hour, with full fuel load.
6	One hour cross country. (Note: The vast difference in ground speeds between the Me 262 and, for example, the He lll made this crucial, for pilots could easily get disoriented.)
7 & 8	One hour in formation flying. (Again crucial, because of the vastly different acceleration and deceleration characteristics of a jet fighter. In a piston engine fighter in formation, a slight movement of the throttle brings about an almost immediate corresponding movement in the airplane; in a jet of the time, either advancing or retarding the throttle did not produce immediate results, so everything had to be anticipated.)
9	Five firing passes at a ground target.

Anyone familiar with British or U.S. training during the period will recognize that this is almost not a program at all, but still it was the best that could be done in view of the limited instructors, limited aircraft, and limited fuel.

Thus, by the time the early development models of engines had been attached to the approximately 315 Me 262's delivered to the *Luftwaffe,* a school was in being. Maximum production from the course must have been limited, perhaps as little as 14 or 20 pilots per month depending upon in-commission rates, flying weather, accidents and so on. This was in December 1944, and was clearly too little to stem the tide of Allied air superiority.

A detailed listing of all of the various subtypes of the Me 262 will be found in Appendix A. Photos of most of these appear throughout the book. In the main, however, production concentrated on the Me 262 A-la *Schwalbe* (Swallow) and the

---

8. From "German Me 262 Fighter, A Collection of Data from Various Sources", ATI 40389, Defense Documentation Center, Alexandria, Va.

Germany's revolutionary jet fighter was produced in two main versions. This is the Me 262A-1A Schwalbe fighter belonging to Jagdgeschwader 7. (Photo Courtesy John Underwood)

The other principal version was the Me 262A-2a fighter bomber, the Sturmvogel (Stormbird). Two 250 Kg (approximately 550 pound) bombs are shown attached to streamlined pylons. The weight and drag of the bombs reduced the Me 262's performance, but the aircraft was successful, within its limited scope, as a bomber. (Messerschmitt Archiv)

Me 262 A-2a *Sturmvogel* (Stormbird). (The Me 262 had other nicknames, too, including "Turbo," "Maple" and "Silver.")[9] The initial principal difference was in the attachment of bomb racks in streamlined fairings under the *Sturmvogel's* nose. The racks, of which there were two main types, could carry a variety of weapons, up to and including two 500 kg bombs, or a single 1,000 kg bomb.*

As production went on, changes were introduced into both the *Schwalbe* and the *Sturmvogel* as a result of operational experience. Additional effort was frittered away on developments which had almost no chance of being brought to fruition in the light of the war situation. But the main thrust of production was remarkable for the time, with about 239 bombers and 741 fighters actually being accepted by the *Luftwaffe*, the remainder of the production effort either going to experimental work, or being destroyed prior to acceptance.

Let us now turn to the operational requirements and actual deployment of the Me 262, so that we can take a close look at individual variants of the aircraft, and determine what pilots' options, both Allied and Axis, there really were.

9. From "German Me 262 Fighter".
* Normal load was either two 250 kg bombs or one 500 kg bomb.—A.G.

The Me 262 at War

Few aircraft can have had as swift a change in prospects during their development life as did the Me 262. Born at a time when Germany was riding high, the 262 was developed under the most difficult wartime conditions. Instead of the normal process in which well tested aircraft are brought into operational use only after a long work-up by first line squadrons, the Me 262 was flung into the cauldron of war before it was really ready.

The Germans had established a test detachment at Lechfield under the command of *Hauptmann* Thierfelder in December 1943, six months before the Jumo 004B engine had been frozen for production. The unit was supposed to train pilots and develop operational tactics, and in the course of this made interceptions of the Lockheed P-38 Lightnings and de Havilland Mosquitos which had previously flown with impunity over Germany on high altitude reconnaissance. Three victories were achieved by this unit before the Allies had their first concrete evidence that the radical jet fighter was being used operationally.

In an oft-quoted RAF Intelligence Report, No. 2256, by Wing Commander G. E. F. Proctor, the first reported Allied encounter with the Me 262 occurred on July 25, 1944, over Munich.

The Mosquito, flown by Flt. Lt. A. E. Wall, with Pilot Officer A. S. Lobban as navigator, was circling at 30,000 feet taking oblique photographs when an enemy aircraft was observed about 400 yards astern. Wall immediately applied full power, and, by diving to 28,000 feet, achieved 412 mph True Air Speed, more than enough to get away from any known German fighter at that altitude. The enemy aircraft, however, had no difficulty following, and a turning dog fight followed. Unable to escape, Wall turned five times into the attacking Me 262, evading until he was able to dive away into some cloud cover and escape.

The report of the combat alarmed Allied Intelligence, naturally, and increased attention was given to reports of new German "wonder" aircraft.

Hauptmann Thierfelder was killed in a crash and command was turned over to the Austrian ace, *Major* Walter Nowotny, former commander of the famous I./JG 54 "Green Hearts." As Me 262 deliveries increased, the unit became *Kommando Nowotny*, with 40 aircraft assigned, and was based near Osnabrueck.

This photo, taken at Achmer during the Spring of 1945, shows an Me 262 A-2a of Kampfgeschwader 51 "Edelweis" Note the code letter "Y" on the fuselage. (Messerschmitt-Bolkow-Blohm GMBM)

Nowotny, whose brilliant career on the Eastern front had made him a *Gruppenkommandeur* at age 24, with 256 victories and the Knight's Cross with Diamonds, had his new group operational by October 3, 1944, for use against U.S. bomber formations. Despite his leadership, the difficulties under which the aircraft were operating and the failure to arrive at effective tactics limited the unit's success.

The Allies enjoyed such air superiority that they were able to put combat air patrols over known jet airfields, so that the Messerschmitt Me 262's could be attacked during their vulnerable takeoffs and landings. The tactic was called "rat catching." The Germans countered first by having Nowotny's old outfit, J.G. 54, flying top cover during these periods. This was an unprofitable situation analogous to the escorting of Messerschmitt Bf 110 fighters by Bf 109's during the Battle of Britain, and one that the *Luftwaffe* could ill afford. Later jet airfields were encircled with enormous belts of anti-aircraft weapons, which made it too hazardous for Allied fighters to risk. The *"Turbos"* would land under a literal canopy of flak.

Nowotny was killed on November 8th, 1944. He had taken off to intercept a formation of American bombers, and his garbled radio transmissions indicated that he had made three kills, then suffered an engine flame out, possibly from combat damage. He reported that he was being attacked, and hit; his aircraft plunged out of the clouds, straight into the ground. *Kommando Nowotny* had already lost 26 aircraft, which oddly enough, exactly equalled the total of their successes, 22 confirmed and four probable kills. Their leader's death forced a reorganization, for the unit had been bled white.

The Sturmvogel in another of its myriad camouflage patterns. The streamlined pylons enclosed the bomb shackles and were called "Wikingerschiff" because of their viking ship shape. (Messerschmitt Archiv)

The sleek shark shape of the Me 262 shows up well here. Note that only two cannon are fitted. (Messerschmitt-Bolkow-Blohm GMBH)

Given the difficult conditions under which the Germans were operating, it is not surprising that accidents caused more casualties than combat. Heavily laden aircraft had to take off and land from bomb-pocked runways; materials were inferior, and parts were hard to obtain; labor was less skilled at that stage of the war, and the mechanics were not yet familiar with the special requirements for jet aircraft.

Even in the closing days of the war, Germany's famed bureaucracy kept working, and statistics revealed that 34% of accidents were the result of undercarriage failure, 33% the result of engine failure, and 10% the result of the tail plane failing due to excessive "G" forces.*

In the meantime, the Messerschmitt Me 262A-2a fighter bombers had entered operational service in August 1944 when *Kampfgeschwader* 51, the "Edelweiss", converted from twin engine Messerschmitt Me 410's to the new jet. Commanded by *Major* Schenk, Kg 51 epitomized the confusion of the Nazi leadership. On the

* Pilot error was at the root of many of these.—A.G.

Me 262 program, German bomber pilots, highly skilled in formation and instrument flying, were given the best fighters in the world to make pinprick bombing attacks against the hordes of Allied armies approaching in the West. The correct tactic, of course, well known to Luftwaffe fighter leaders, would have been to give sufficient training to fighter pilots to enable them to handle the Me 262, to have given fighter conversion training to the bomber pilots, and to have employed the Me 262 solely as a fighter.

Still the Me 262 was surprisingly effective as a bomber, considering that the addition of bomb racks, releases, and other related equipment had been an entirely *ad hoc* measure designed as a sop to Hitler's requirements. The original tactics were for a single jet to fly at 25,000 feet on the approach to the target, then, at the initial point, begin a dive which would end at 18,000 feet with bomb release. Night attacks were made at lower altitudes, 10,000 to 12,000 feet, with a dive to only 8,000 feet. As could be expected, actual operational experience developed better ways to use the 262, and by the end of the war it was doctrine that shallow dive bombing was best done by units of four aircraft abreast, at about 15,000 feet altitude (or lower) with about 100 yards lateral intervals. With either one 500 or two 250 kg bombs, accuracy equal to that obtained by the conventional F.W. 190 was achieved.[1]

The target was approached until it disappeared from sight under the left or right jet engine, and then the dive began. The dive was made at an angle of 30 degrees, using the ordinary Revi sight for aiming. Speeds were limited to about 850 to 900 km/h, with the jets throttled back to about 6,000 feet. Bombs were released from an altitude of 3,000 to 3,500 feet. Pilots had to be sure to have the rear auxiliary tank empty before pull up, or the aircraft could pitch-up uncontrollably and break up.

Generally, the Me 262 was not successful as a ground strafer, because of the low muzzle velocity of the MK 108 cannon, and the 360 rounds of ammunition carried were not enough to cover much area. In addition, the Me 262 was not well armored against ground fire.

One of the last desperation efforts of the Me 262 was a revival of air to air bombing techniques. Dr. Kortum of Zeiss had developed a new sight called the *Gegner Pfeil Visier* (Flight Path Pointer) GPV-1 of which about 20 models were produced. The sight computed the values for the relative speeds of the Me 262 and the bomber formation, using ballistic figures for the type of bombs being carried.

Four Me 262's were to fly in echelon, with about 30 yards interval, and to pass 3,000 feet above the enemy bomber formation. Each Me 262 had a colored stripe painted along the nose, set at 15 degrees below the horizontal. The attacking jets would dive from about 3,000 yards out, with bombs released when the bombers were about 600 yards away. The Me 262 would then break and climb for home.[2]

---

1. From "German Me 262 Fighter".   2. From "German Me 262 Fighter".

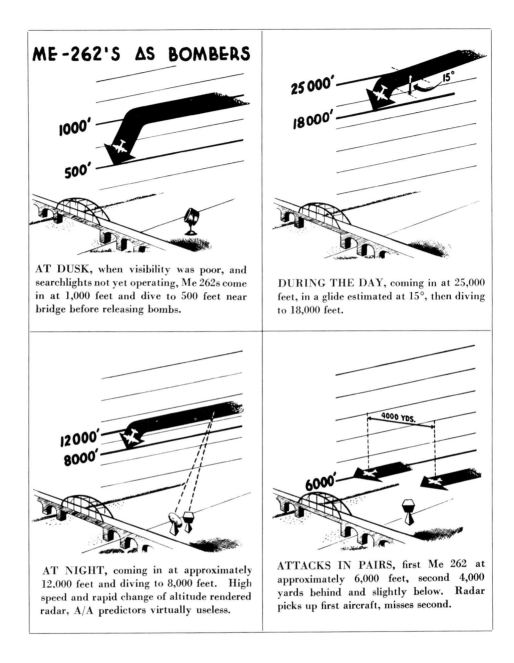

ME-262'S AS BOMBERS

AT DUSK, when visibility was poor, and searchlights not yet operating, Me 262s come in at 1,000 feet and dive to 500 feet near bridge before releasing bombs.

DURING THE DAY, coming in at 25,000 feet, in a glide estimated at 15°, then diving to 18,000 feet.

AT NIGHT, coming in at approximately 12,000 feet and diving to 8,000 feet. High speed and rapid change of altitude rendered radar, A/A predictors virtually useless.

ATTACKS IN PAIRS, first Me 262 at approximately 6,000 feet, second 4,000 yards behind and slightly below. Radar picks up first aircraft, misses second.

From AAF intelligence report No.45-102, 10 February 1945.

While all of these bombing methods were frittering away the little strength remaining to the *Luftwaffe,* the Me 262's used as fighters were encountering varied degrees of success.

Jagdgeschwader 7 (Nowotny), under the command of *Oberst* Johannes Steinhoff, was formed in December 1944; it stayed in operation until the end of the war, and the Museum aircraft is from that unit. The *III Gruppe* of JG 7, with the addition of the staff element, was able to maintain a full complement of 45 aircraft in action, and

This aircraft, work number 130 167, was used as an experimental prototype at the Rechlin test center. Note how canopy hinges in a manner similar to Messerschmitt Bf109; entire canopy, except for windscreen, could be jettisoned in an emergency.

A Schwalbe from Kommando Nowothy which formed the basis for Jagdgeschwader 7. This photo is often seen retouched to be an "air to air shot." (Messerschmitt Archiv)

This Schwalbe landed in Switzerland and was interned. Many years later it was returned to Germany and now, fully restored, occupies a place of pride in the fine Deutches Museum in Munich.

reportedly claimed more than 400 aircraft, including 300 four engine bombers shot down. While this claim is almost certainly too high, it was performance like this, in the last five months of the war, which is the best support for the opinions of such luminaries as Lt. General Galland, who feels that the introduction of the Messerschmitt Me 262 some 18 months earlier would have influenced the conduct of the air war.

As the war ground inexorably to its close, other units, principally former bomber organizations, were converted to the Messerschmitt Me 262. Despite all efforts, the shortages of equipment and the primacy of the Allied air forces prevented them achieving effective operational status. A list of these units is provided in Appendix C.

One unit which did achieve operational status, was as legendary a group as the Richthofen Circus, the Lafayette Escadrille and the Eagle Squadron all rolled into one. It was *Jagdverband* 44, the elite of the elite.

Generalleutenant Galland, former *General der Jagdflieger*, the top post in the German fighter command, had been fired by *Reichsmarschall* Goering for his repeated insistence on telling the truth, and was told to form his own fighter squadron.

Thus, in the dying days of World War II, a man who had sprinted to the forefront of German fighter pilots, scoring 97 victories, and had spent "the best years of the war" as a staff officer, combating ineptitude and corruption within, was relegated once again to a squadron. Yet what a squadron. Of its members, no less than 10 held the Knight's Cross; all were experienced fighter pilots who flowed to Galland in a search for leadership and an opportunity to fly the Me 262, for one last chance at air superiority. In it Galland scored seven more times bringing his victory total to 104.

JV 44, a "Squadron of Experts" was composed of men like Steinhoff (176 victories), *Major* Gerd Barkhorn (301 victories), *Major* Erich Hohagen (57 victories), *Major* Walter Krupinski (197 victories), *Oberst* Guenther Luetzow (108 victories) and others of similar skills. They were intelligent men, with absolutely no illusions about the eventual outcome of the war or the shortcomings of their own government. But they were soldiers and patriots, exhilarated by the chance to fly the *Turbo*, and willing to contribute everything even at a time when their contribution could do nothing.

JV 44 trained with JV 7, then moved to Munchen-Riem on March 31, 1945, for a last ditch effort. The war had only 39 days to go, yet JV 44 was to make history.

The general debilitation of the Luftwaffe was not felt at JV 44, for aircraft from other units were funnelled to it as the war ebbed, till at last there were more planes than there were pilots to fly them. And the Me 262 had been considerably improved by the addition of R4M air to air rockets. Designed by Kurt Heber, the 55 mm rockets were mounted in groups of 12 under each wing, in very simple wooden rocket launchers. German technique called for the R4M armed Me 262 to approach bomber formations from the rear, and fire the entire battery of 24 rockets to saturate the area in which a bomber would be flying. The Me 262 could then return to engage other aircraft in the formation with its cannon.

Galland led his JV 44 into battle until April 26th when, after a successful assault on a Martin Marauder bomber formation (one in which the old hunter, the old pro, had forgotten to release the safety on his rockets, and had to use his cannon armament!), he was attacked by the escorting P-47 Thunderbolts. The Me 262 was badly hit and Galland was wounded; he managed to plant the aircraft on the runway at a roaring 175 kmph, and survive a formation of Republic P-47 Thunderbolts that were strafing the field.[3] Galland went to a hospital, but JV 44 fought on until it was overrun on May 3, 1945. The unit, with its elite personnel, had scored 50 victories during its short existence.

3. "The Preliminary Interrogation of One of GAF Most Famous Pilots: Galland", APWIU(1st TACAF), 45/1945

The simple appearance of the R4M rocket installation belies their deadly efficiency. Normal load was a group of 12 rockets under each wing. They were fired simultaneously at a range of about 650 yards and would saturate an area about the size of a B-17 formation. (Messerschmitt Archiv)

Pilots' Views on the Me 262

Because of the almost intolerable conditions under which the Me 262 was developed and deployed as a fighter, the *Luftwaffe* was never able to create more than the most rudimentary tactics for the employment of its fantastic new weapon. Contrary to past years, when tactical doctrine was rigidly controlled, each Me 262 unit expanded upon its limited training instructions and developed methods of its own. JG 7, for example, chose to fly missions in the standard *Luftwaffe* four plane element, the *Schwarm*. JV 44 on the other hand, reverted to the classic pre-war three ship formation the *Ketten*, partially because the flying characteristics of the Me 262 made it difficult for more than three to maintain close formation.[4] Despite the prevailing conditions, as many as 24 aircraft could be scrambled in just five minutes, three ships at a time.

Normally in attacking bombers, formations of nine aircraft flying three elements of three were used. One element would lead and the other two would be on the flanks, higher, and slightly back. About 300 to 450 feet distance was maintained between aircraft, and about 900 feet between elements, a loose formation which provided good visibility and accommodated for the lack of maneuverability at altitude.

4. From "German Me 262 Fighter".

After years of success with the finger-four formation, the reversion to three ship elements was only possible because the speed of the Me 262 made mutual protection almost unnecessary.

The general plan was for each *Staffel* of nine to 12 aircraft to attack an individual bomber group. The *Staffel* would approach from behind the formation and begin the attack from about three miles out, diving to gain speed. Then the Me 262 would form into columns of three aircraft each, flying 500 yards below and 1,500 yards behind the bombers to get position, much as receiver aircraft position themselves behind tankers before pulling in for refueling. The last 1,000 yards of the attack would be flown straight and level at about 850 kmph. The ideal attack was considered to be almost, but not quite, dead astern. At 650 yards the wingspan of a B-17 would just fill the Revi sights, and the 24 R4M rockets would be fired. The Me 262 would close to about 150 yards and then begin to climb through the formation, passing as close as possible above the top level of bombers to make it hard for the gunners to track them. The *Turbos* avoided flying under the formation because of the danger that debris from damaged bombers might be sucked into the jet intakes.

The Me 262's did not ordinarily reassemble after an attack because of the fuel required. They could either return for individual attacks, or simply depart the scene in a shallow dive, outrunning any Allied fighters around.

The *Schwalbe* was less successful in its attempts against Allied fighters, primarily because the jet pilots would often forget to utilize the principal advantage, speed and climb, and attempt to dogfight. A canny Me 262 pilot could accept or refuse combat as he chose, unless, of course, he was surprised. The Allied pilots were very aggressive, however, and always sought to suck the Me 262's into turning engagements. Experienced jet pilots would play this game for only about one third of a turn before applying power and climbing away.

The best hunting the Me 262 enjoyed was against fighter bombers, for its speed advantage was greatest at lower altitudes, and the fighter bombers were usually encumbered with external ordnance. The Me 262's would whistle along at tree top level, jet exhausts blasting the leaves, and then, when spotting the Allied "Jabos" silhouetted against the clouds, climb and attack from underneath, an unorthodox tactic possible only because of their superb performance.

Time has not diminished the somewhat fierce affection felt by the privileged few German pilots who flew the Me 262 in its final, glorious moments, and it is interesting to note that, professionals as they are, they can recall vividly both the *Turbo's* advantages and deficiencies.

Galland, still an overwhelmingly impressive individual even with graying hair and in civilian clothes, was and is absolutely convinced that the Me 262 could have been brought to operational status early enough to have had an effect on the air war. His remarks after his first flight have been often quoted, the most apt being, "It felt like angels were pushing." He felt that the Me 262 was neither harder nor easier to fly than the Bf 109 or Focke Wulfe Fw 190, but that it could have been improved if it had had more powerful and reliable jet engines, more R4M rockets (there were plans to place 24 on each side, doubling the fire power), gyroscopic gunsights, ejection seats, and a better electric starter.

Galland also noted that the workmanship on the Me 262 went down towards the end of the war, as it did on all aircraft.

Major Rudolph Sinner also replied to my questionnaire, sent through the German Society of Fighter Pilots to ex-262 pilots. Like Nowotny, Sinner was born in Austria and after the *Anschluss* joined the *Luftwaffe.* He shot down 39 aircraft, three in the Me 262 when he was in JG-7. One of the "anonymous aces" of the *Luftwaffe,* Sinner's brilliant career would have been a legend in any other air force in the world, for he flew 390 missions, engaged in aerial combat 96 times, was shot down 12 times, wounded five times, and once landed behind enemy lines to rescue a friend. Yet he did not win the Knight's Cross, and regards himself as "an ordinary soldier."

He liked the Me 262 because of its speed and firepower, which was almost 400 kmh faster than his old favorite, the Bf 109G and had three times the punch. He felt that the *Turbo* enabled German pilots to catch reconnaissance planes that had previously been invulnerable, to attack the heavily defended bomber formations with little risk, and to be able to repeat attacks individually because the Me 262 could evade enemy fighters. More than anything else, it gave the German pilot the sense that he had the initiative in aerial combat, an essential part of being a fighter pilot.

Yet Sinner recalls some disadvantages, too. He felt the Me 262 was too vulnerable during takeoff and landing, because of the greater period of time and distance required. He realized the starting procedure was considerably more complicated than for the piston engine aircraft, and that the jet engines were still not as reliable and much shorter lived than the piston type. The exigencies of war also made the Me 262's greater requirements for field size, ground organization, engineering, flying safety and tactical management difficult to fulfill. Finally, Sinner notes that the Me 262 was limited in its diving ability, for its clean airframe could easily slip past the critical Mach number, and there was no way to prevent a sudden pitch-up with possibly catastrophic results.

As far as improvements to the aircraft, Sinner would have liked to have seen more use of drop tanks, a better starter system, using starter carts rather than the built-in Riedel starter, and more use of rockets to assist takeoffs.

Johannes "Macky" Steinhoff's book, *The Last Chance,* is a revealing insight into the "revolt of the *Kommodores,*" the unsuccessful attempt to wrest *Luftwaffe* leadership from Goering. He also recounts the desperate attempts to develop the correct tactics for the Me 262, and is in a better position than most to carefully evaluate the aircraft. Trained to fly in 1934 in the German Naval Aviation school at Kiel, he transferred to the *Luftwaffe* in 1936. He scored 149 victories in Russia, and 27 on the Western front, the last five of these in the Me 262. From 1939 to 1945 he flew

993 combat missions and was shot down 12 times. On April 18, 1945. his overladen Me 262 crashed on takeoff and he was badly burned. With characteristic fortitude, Steinhoff came back to rise to the highest position in the postwar *Luftwaffe* before retiring. One of the first jet aces, after the war he flew such sophisticated aircraft as the North American F-86, Grumman F-11, Lockheed F-104, McDonnell Douglas F-4, and many others.

His comments on the questionnaire reveal this background. He fully appreciated all of the magnificent qualities of the Me 262, including its speed, climbing ability, heavy firepower and ability to either engage or disengage in combat at will. But, more important, he recognized the advantages of the Me 262's low pressure tires, which permitted it to operate from grass strips, its mechanical controls which were relatively invulnerable to fire, and its very heavy armament. And he saw, as few others did, that the greatest disadvantage of the Me 262 was its lack of speed brakes or maneuvering flaps.* With engines as sensitive to stall as the Junkers Jumo 004B were, the requirement to reduce power to decrease speed was a severe handicap. With good speed brakes, engine power could have been left up, and speed controlled aerodynamically.

Generalmajor Erich Hohagen agrees completely with Steinhoff in this regard. Hohagen, who had 57 victories prior to joining JV 44, regards the Me 262 as "the absolute fulfillment of a flying career, the biggest step since the Wright brothers...." Like Steinhoff, he feels that the addition of dive brakes would have made a much better airplane, as would an improved hydraulic system.

It was somehow fitting that the Me 262's operations would come to a halt in the hands of the men best equipped to use them. The fire of experience had turned the pilots of JV 44 into the best combat pilots in the world; the fortunes of war put the Me 262 in their hands at a time when it could be only a symbolic epitaph for the *Luftwaffe,* an air arm which had come in four years from nothing to be the most feared in the world, and in a further six to nothing again.

The Me 262
from the
Allied Point of View

It is incredible that as important as the Me 262 was to the planners, leaders, and top pilots of the *Luftwaffe*, it was just a little added spice to the humdrum side of an almost-won air war being experienced by Allied fighter pilots in late 1944 and 1945.

This difference in attitude is evident in the almost raucous accounts of combat recorded by American pilots, who found the speed and dash of the Me 262 to be a tonic. As one reads report after report of encounters, the single impression that comes through is the universal inclination of the American pilots to engage the jets at whatever costs, and their absolute indifference to the distinct speed and firepower advantage of the Me 262's. It was a confidence born of superior training, excellent equipment, massive numbers, and a long experience at winning.

* Adolf Galland disagrees with Steinhoff noting that he did everything to prevent the development of speed brakes because their application would have increased the acceleration time.

The view of the Me 262 that Allied fighter pilots liked best: from above and behind. Note Republic P-47 in front of Me 262. (U.S.A.A.F.)

The following account of a single action is taken from Kenn C. Rust and William N. Hess' article "The German Jets and the U.S. Army Air Force" from Volume 8, Number III of the *American Aviation Historical Society Journal.* It illustrates the conditions under which the Me 262 had to engage in combat, and the lustful joy with which American pilots sought the *Schwalbe* out.

"Weather conditions on November 1 limited attacks by the 8th AF which dispatched only 318 heavy bombers against two synthetic oil plants at Gelsenkirchen and the Hindenburg Bridge over the Rhine at Ruedesheim. B-17's of the 1st Division made the Gelsenkirchen attack with little opposition and were returning to England via Holland under P-51 escort when they were intercepted by a lone Me 262. The jet, Werke Number 110 386, piloted by *Oberfaehnrich* Banzhaff, approached the bombers and fighters at 38,000 feet. At 1412 he put his machine into a dive toward the top cover fighters flying at 32,000 feet below him, a section of the 20th Fighter Group. He came down in a perfect bounce on Yellow Flight of the 20th, fired in a 30 degree

A series of gun camera photos reportedly taken during a single engagement. (U.S. Air Force)

dive on the Number 4 man, 1st Lt. Dennis J. Alison, and shot him down in flames. Then Banzhaff continued his dive over the Fortress formations but was immediately pursued by P-51s of the 20th Fighter Group.

All of this action was seen by members of the 56th Fighter Group, who had been escorting Liberators with their P-47's, and they immediately turned toward the German jet. At the same time, P-51's of the 352nd Fighter Group also went after Banzhaff. It seemed that every American fighter plane in the sky was in a mad scramble to get in a shot at him.

Banzhaff continued his dive to about 10,000 feet then made a climbing 180 degree turn at full throttle, taking up a northerly heading toward the Zuider Zee just above a layer of clouds. If he had gone into the clouds at this point, he would have been safe from the aircraft of the three groups chasing him, but he apparently felt his speed would allow him to out-race his pursuers. However, in making his 180 degree turn, he gave the diving P-51's and P-47's an opportunity to cut him off. Both Mustangs and Thunderbolts opened fire hitting the jet on the left side of the fuselage and the left wing. Lt. Flowers of the 20th, pulling over 72 inches of mercury at 3,000 RPM, scored hits. So did Lt. Gerbe of the 352nd. So did three other pilots. Lt. Groce, White 4 of the 63rd Squadron, 56th Group, called his mates on the radio, "Spread it out and we'll get him if he turns." A moment later the hounded Banzhaff made a climbing turn to the left and put himself slightly above Lt. Groce's flight. Groce pulled his nose right through the Me 262, in order to get enough deflection, firing all the time. The jet's right engine burst into flames, the Me 262 fell off into a spin, and *Oberfaehnrich* Banzhaff bailed out.

Six pilots from the three groups involved in this flight over Holland from the Enschede to Zwolle areas claimed the Me 262, but subsequently the victory was awarded on a share basis between Lts. Groce and Gerbe."

The first recorded victory over a Me 262 came on August 28, 1944, when Major Joseph Myers and Lt. M. D. Croy bounced a low flying *Turbo* near Brussels and shot it down. The aircraft, a Me 262A-2a flown by *Feldwebel* "Ronny" Lauer, crash landed.

In the months that followed, the Messerschmitt Me 262 was committed piecemeal to attacks against the huge bomber and fighter formations, and however great their individual performance superiority they were unable to cope with the gangs of P-51's and P-47's which roamed the German skies and were apt to attack from any direction, at any point in the flight.

Detailed analysis of the records of combat from August 1944 to May 1945 indicates that the Me 262 units suffered more losses than they inflicted. Eighth Air Force records indicate that 52 bombers and 10 fighters were lost to jets during the period, while more than 200 jets were destroyed.* Even though these figures may be exaggerated, they at least set the terms upon which the Me 262's combat performance has to be evaluated.

Probably the principal effect of the Me 262 was to hasten Allied development of jet fighters, principally, the Gloster *Meteor* and the Lockheed P-80 *Shooting Star*. The threat of the jet did divert some effort in strategic bombing, and the requirement to watch continuously over the jet landing fields undoubtedly represented a drain on Allied resources. The practical fact of the matter is, however, that the Allied dominance of the air was so complete that no change in aerial tactics was required of either bombers or fighters. The jets were simply engaged as they appeared in the classic manner—turn into them when they attack, bounce them if they are below you, get as close as you can and fire with everything you've got.

None of this diminishes in any way the brilliance of the Me 262 as an aircraft or the skill and bravery of the pilots who flew them. It simply illustrates the total air superiority of the Allies, which was still building in 1944, and could, with the introduction of the B-29 and jet fighters in late 1945, have grown into even more towering proportions. The Me 262 was a fascinating sidebar on the war, nothing more.

* Including those on the ground.—A.G.

56

Watson literally charmed cooperation from the confused, depressed German Luftwaffe personnel. (Major General Harold E. Watson)

CHAPTER 6

The National Air and Space Museum's Me 262

Colonel (Later Major General) Harold E. Watson led "Operation Lusty", an almost piratical foray into Germany to capture flyable examples of the latest aircraft types. Watson's unique combination of engineering talent, test pilot experience and engaging personality enabled him to work well with the just defeated Germane pilots and crew men who were vital to get the aircraft airworthy. (Courtesy Major General Harold E. Watson, USAF, Retired)

The most amazing thing about the acquisition of the Museum's Me 262 is that there has never been a movie made about it. The aircraft was acquired under circumstances that could have existed only in those joyous, confused months of May and June 1945, when the Nazi *Götterdämmerung* had played out its last doleful notes, and sensible men of good will began to appear on all sides.

A young man who could easily have played the leading role, Colonel Harold E. Watson, was the star of "Operation Lusty," an imaginative project to acquire quickly flyable examples of the *Luftwaffe's* latest aircraft and get them back to the United States for tests. The principal aim was to determine if there was something to be learned for use in the war against the Japanese, but there was a secondary urgency, a desire if not to keep the new types from the hands of the Russians, (for this was almost impossible) at least to learn as much from the Germans as the Russians would learn.

Watson gathered about him a group of experienced young fighter pilots forming an Air Force Intelligence Team that would be informally known as "Watson's Whizzers" and as the "USAAF's first jet squadron."

The entire operation was like a little D-Day in reverse; Watson's task was to seek out from German airfields the aircraft most wanted for evaluation by Wright Field experts in the United States; he was to stalk these fields, gather up the aircraft along with the German technicians who could service them, sufficient spare parts for their continued operation, and then sweep them back to Cherbourg where they could be placed on a carrier for the trip home. All the necessary trucks, cranes, billets, mess facilities, and personnel had to be provided from commands that were not really sure what the team's secret mission was.

Watson was a natural choice for leader; an imaginative engineer at Wright Field before the war, and a test pilot with thousands of hours, Watson also had a rare organizational ability and a flair for command. He was able to solicit assistance from bored American staff officers whose principal aim was either to go home to civilian life, or to Japan to fight again; from defeated German technicians and soldiers whose emotions ranged from depression at their surrender to a patriotic desire to help the Americans instead of the Russians; from French officers who wished to celebrate the

victory on every occasion; and even from sharp British teams doing the same task he was doing, and from whom he managed to "steal" one of his targets.

In June 1945 the Museum's Me 262 was located at Lechfeld, in Bavaria. Lechfeld, site of the original Test Detachment (*Erprobungskommando*) which brought the *Schwalbe* into combat, was then a virtual dumping ground for surviving *Luftwaffe* units. The field was literally filled with exotic prizes of war, including Heinkel He 162 *Volksjägers,* Arado Ar 234's; and so on.

Flying in three C-47's that had been so equipped with rations, tents, tools and so on as to be almost self sufficient, Watson used his charm as well as his military authority to induce German personnel to identify the most airworthy aircraft, make necessary repairs, and ferret out spare parts, operations manuals, etc.

There were ten Me 262's selected at Lechfeld for removal to the United States, including a Me 262B-1a two-seat trainer. Two German test pilots were on hand, and with suitable inducement, they agreed to check out the American pilots.

Lt. Roy Brown, one of Watson's Whizzers recalled the training process in a recent letter to writer Jeff Ethell. Brown, now a prosperous businessman, but then a hot shot P-47 pilot with a chemical engineering background, was typical of the personnel selected for Watson's elite group.

Brown's checkout was relatively simple. He was given instruction in starting and stopping the engine several times, then made one trip around the field in the two-

German fields were littered with abandoned aircraft at the end of the war. This Me 262, like many others wound up on its nose as a prelude to the scrap heap. (Roy W. Brown Photo)

Only a relatively few of the two seat trainer version of the Me 262 were built. Two were available for "Watson's Whizzers." This is "Vera" (believed to be renamed "Willy" later). (Roy W. Brown Photo)

A high speed low pass at Lechfeld. (Roy W. Brown)

Ludwig "Willie" Hoffman, former Messerschmitt test pilot, gave most of "Watsons Whizzers" their first experience in a jet. The pilots found the two seat Me 262 B-1a easy to fly, once proper engine control techniques were learned. Hoffman was scheduled to become a Bachem Natter pilot; he had already flown it once.
(Roy W. Brown Photo)

Already decorated with U.S. insignia and unit motto "Feuding 54th A.D. Squadron," this Me 262 taxies in after landing at Lechfeld, Germany, June 1945. (Roy W. Brown)

Emergencies were suprisingly uncommon despite the chaotic conditions in Germany on June 1945. This Me 262 is making a fly past to check its landing gear which had failed to retract. (Roy W. Brown Photo)

U.S. maintenance practices were not too dissimilar from German, and a standard retraction test was the same at Lechfeld, Germany, as at Wright Field, Ohio. (Roy W. Brown Photo)

June 10, 1945.
Messerschmitt Me 262's lined up at Lechfeld for the flight to Melun, France. (Roy W. Brown Photo)

Lt. Roy Brown's plane, "Connie The Sharp Article." These names were not chosen by pilots of Watson's Whizzers. Note bulge on nose which faired in the RB 50/30 cameras of this Me 262 A-1a/U3.

seat Me 262. Brown recalls that the plane was stable and easy to land. The German pilots had warned them to land with a little power, i.e. with the engines running at a little more than idle speed, so that a sudden power application could be made more easily.

Watson supervised the checkout process, and in the meantime delivered the first Me 262 by flying over the proposed route from Lechfeld to Melun, France. It was to be a VFR (Visual Flight Rules), medium altitude, non-stop trip, except for the two-seater, which had to land and refuel at Stuttgart.

Prior to takeoff, the German national markings were painted over and U.S. insignia applied. Each aircraft carried a woman's name painted on the nose, and Brown recalls these as already having been applied when Watson's group arrived to pick the planes up.

The planes were lined up as follows:

ME 262	PILOT	TAKE-OFF TIME (June 10, 1945)
Vera	Mr. Hoffman	0925 (Two-seat trainer, German pilot)
Joanne	Capt. Hillis	0930
Pauline	Lt. Anspach	0945
Julie	Lt. Holt	1000
Doris	Capt. Dahlstrom	1015
Connie	Lt. Brown	1030
Marge	Mr. Bowers	1045 (German pilot)
Beverly Ann	Lt. Strobell	1100
Wilma Jeanne	Col. Watson	1115 (Had 50 mm Cannon)

"Connie" was renamed "Pick II" by Lt. Roy W. Brown, shown here. He had named his Thunderbolt "Pick", an affectionate nickname for his wife. (Roy W. Brown Photo)

Watson's flight plan was simple; the planes were to fly southwest on a heading of 222 degrees magnetic to Eschede, about 198 miles away; to turn further south to 229 degrees magnetic for 138 miles to Le Oulot, then back to 220 degrees magnetic for the final 179 miles to Melun. Total distance was 515 miles, with a time enroute of 1 hour and 30 minutes, using about 4,000 liters of fuel.

Brown described his flight, his first crosscountry in a jet, as a real thrill; the *Schwalbe* was a pilot's airplane, responsive, fast and smooth.

By June 11, 1945, the most important phase of Watson's mission had been completed; ten Messerschmitt Me 262's were safely at Melun, ten crew chiefs had been trained, and five truck loads of spare parts, tools and special maintenance equipment were on hand. Six Americans had been trained to fly the Me 262, and two German test pilots had joined them for the task.

At Melun, the planes were serviced, repainted and prepared for the flight to Cherbourg. The girls names on the nose were replaced with others preferred by the pilots; Lt. Brown's "Connie the Sharp Article" became "Pick II"; his P-47 had been "Pick," his wife's nickname.

General Carl A. "Tooey" Spaatz inspected the collection of aircraft at Melun on June 27th, and three Me 262's were demonstrated in the air. One of these was very possibly the Museum's aircraft, for the operational orders indicate that Me 262, coded 888, was one of the three primary aircraft slated for the fly-by. This number was later found on the Museum's Me 262.

The aircraft were subsequently flown to Cherbourg. One, the former "Wilma Jeanne", was newly named "Happy Hunter." It suffered an engine malfunction; the resultant vibration forced the German pilot, Ludwig Hoffman, to bail out. He did so successfully, and this was the only plane lost during the entire "Operation Lusty."

At Cherbourg, the planes were "pickled," put on lighters, and then lifted to the Royal Navy's aircraft carrier, H.M.S. Reaper, for a trip to the United States.

The aircraft were offloaded at Newark, then assembled and flown to Freeman Field, Indiana, with one stop enroute at Pittsburgh. At Freeman Field, Indiana, the planes were given "FE" numbers for test purposes with the Museum's aircraft being "FE lll." ("FE" is an abbreviation for foreign equipment).

Oddly enough, to date no one has unearthed the reports of the extensive flight and ground testing conducted at Freeman Field. I have examined at length the records in the Military Record Center at St. Louis concerning Freeman Field activities, and while you can find out everything you do not want to know about the routine events, there is nothing on the flight test activities.

A second Me 262 B-1a was brought to Melun, France in June, 1945. Hoffman is in the process of checking out 1st Lt. William K. Haynes. (Roy W. Brown Photo)

The U. S. pilots were quick to repaint and rename the German aircraft. Note "Watson's Whizzers" insignia on nose. (Major General Harold E. Watson)

66

Towing the Me 262 was
not something to be taken
lightly. Unless the correct
tools were used, the nose
gear could collapse. Metal
items on wing are chocks.

General Carl A. "Tooey"
Spaatz inspected the Me
262 at Melun. Shown here
with Col. Watson and
General McDonald (from
the U.S. Embassy in
London). Spaatz commented
"Wicked" when the
captured Me 262s flashed
overhead.

67

One of the more exotic versons captured at Lechfeld was this Me 262 A-1a (Work Number 130 083), specially modified to carry a 50mm Mauser MK 214 A Cannon. This aircraft was flight tested prior to the war's end, and oddly enough, the cannon installation did not seriously impair the Schwalbe's performance. Only one round could be fired at a time, due to the smoke resulting from firing.

"Wilma Jeanne" was flown to Melun by Colonel Watson, where is was repainted and renamed "Happy Hunter II." Unfortunately this aircraft suffered a severe engine vibration enroute from Melun to Cherbourg, and the German test pilot, Hoffman, had to bail out. It was the only crash of "Operation Lusty". (Major General Harold E. Watson)

The end of the "Happy Hunter II." (Major General Harold E. Watson)

68

Another of the four standard Schwalbe's which had been fitted with the 50mm Cannon. The installation was not flight tested in this aircraft. (Roy W. Brown Photo)

The huge Junkers Ju 290 "Alles Kaput" flown across the Atlantic by Colonel Watson. After its arrival, it was found to have been sabotaged by a bomb set to explode in its wing. Fortunately, it did not go off. (Major General Harold E. Watson)

The aircraft were partially disassembled at Cherbourg, "pickled" with standard preservatives, and placed on the Royal Navy aircraft carrier H.M.S. Reaper for shipment to the U.S. (Roy W. Brown Photo)

FE (Foreign Equipment) 110, a Messerschmitt Me 262, in which Col. Watson almost lost his life in an initial test flight at Freeman Field, Indiana. Immediately, after take off he discovered the elevator controls had been rigged backwards and it required full forward pressure on the stick to keep the plane airborne. (USAF Photo)

Col. Watson, who had flown the huge Junkers Ju 290 "Alles Kaput" across the Atlantic to Wright Field, undertook several test programs at Freeman Field including a harrowing first flight in a Messerschmitt Me 262, FE 110. The elevator controls had been reversed, and he had to use his full strength to keep the plane from diving straight into the ground, flying a long low circuit around the field, just able to stay airborne.

In addition to testing, some of the captured aircraft were used in static displays, notably at Wright Field in October 1945, and Cleveland in early 1946.

Up to this time the Museum aircraft had retained its original fighter type nose; somewhere after this date, and prior to the shipment of Me 262 A-1a/U3, FE 4012, to the Hughes Aircraft Company for rebuilding for tests against the Lockheed XP-80, a "nose job" was performed.

FE 4012 had been brought to the U.S. with a reconnaissance nose, characterized by the bulged streamlined plates over the cameras which were installed. A decision must have been made at Freeman Field that FE 4012 should have a fighter nose for a true comparison test with the Locheed P80A. As the noses were readily interchangeable, a swap was made, and FE 111's fighter nose was attached to FE 4012's fuselage. The latter aircraft subsequently went to Hughes Aircraft for a complete rebuilding. Later it was released for surplus to a ground training school, finally winding up in the possession of its present owner, Ed Maloney's Planes of Fame Museum in California.

71

The Museum Aircraft, FE 111, with its original nose at a postwar display of captured aircraft. (USAF Photo)

Another photo of FE 111 with its "fighter nose." (USAF Photo)

A Me 262 A-1a/U3, FE 4012, with the stream lined fairings over the camera. Photo taken September 30, 1945. (USAF Photo)

FE 111 was given 4012's old nose, and amazingly, there was sufficient regard for its museum potential that the sheet metal fairings necessary to streamline the nose camera's bulge into the aft fuselage were formed, and the JG 7 insignia, which the fairings covered, was carefully repainted.

FE 111 next went to Park Ridge, Illinois, where it joined the rest of the then National Air Museum's collection for a stay until 1950. Then, with the advent of the Korean War and the requirement to move the Park Ridge Collection to Silver Hill, it came East.

The aircraft was so highly prized that it was kept inside for the majority of its 28 year stay at Silver Hill until restoration began.

The detective work involved in determining what the aircraft work number (construction number in American parlance) and who the pilot might have been could not really begin until the restoration process was started. As we shall see in Chapter Seven, the beginning search for information in a restoration process is a time consuming one in which delicate hand sanding, hour after hour, is the only useful method.

Despite intensive search, no clearly defined, absolutely certain work number could be found. The number 500491 was found inside the lower cowling of the left and right engine nacelles, and was reportedly also found on the inside of the nose wheel door at an earlier date. Inasmuch as there was no other number which seemed more logical, and as it was impossible to validate what the correct number would be, 500491 was tentatively adopted. This number falls within a block of numbers suitable for this model of Me 262's.

The aircraft's markings clearly reveal that it belonged to 11th Staffel, Gruppe III of JG 7; as the aircraft carried a very unique set of victory markings, we thought we would be able to determine who the pilot was. Unfortunately, as in the case of

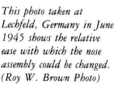

This photo taken at Lechfeld, Germany in June 1945 shows the relative ease with which the nose assembly could be changed. (Roy W. Brown Photo)

Me 262 FE 4012 was shipped with its new nose section to the aircraft division of the Hughes Tool Company in Culver City where it was completely rebuilt. Oddly enough it was refinished with German insignia even though the paint and markings were inaccurate. The FE number was changed to T-2 4012. Howard Hughes reportedly wished to acquire the aircraft. This was probably the best finished Me 262 ever until the Silver Hill restoration. (USAF Photo)

the work number, the results are not definite. We made a number of inquiries, through the German Society of Fighter Pilots, and through the German Embassy. *Hauptmann* Ernst Maison, Traditions Officer of *Jagdesgeschwader* 74 *"Moelders,"* replied that the pilot of NASM's Me 262 was *Oberfeldwebel* Heinz Arnold, who was listed as missing on April 17, 1945.

The basis for the assumption that *Oberfeldwebel* Arnold flew Yellow 7 is not known, but we believe it is based on the victory markings, which show 42 victories over Russian aircraft, and seven over U.S. aircraft. Arnold is shown in other sources as having 40 or 42 victories. It is also possible that Arnold did indeed have his 42 victory record placed on the aircraft, but that victories gained by other pilots were added. In the last two months of the war, it could hardly be expected that either the victory records or the aircraft paint scheme could be kept up to date.

During the restoration process, some evidence of battle damage was found. A bullet had passed through the rear bulkhead of the left wing, forward and through the center web of the main spar. It continued forward, tearing out a small section of the stringer adjacent to the spar, and then bounced against the next stringer before tumbling against the outer upper skin of the wing. A copper jacketed .30 caliber armor piercing bullet was found just aft of the spar.

Another similar bullet path was found aft of the wing in the lower right side of the fuselage.

Both entrance holes had been patched, probably by the Germans prior to the aircraft's capture.

Regardless of its combat history, or who flew it, the NASM Me 262 is a historic aircraft as a type. Perhaps even more important, whoever flew this airplane, or any of the Me 262s in combat, was a brave and worthy foe, and we are pleased to have his aircraft for visitors to admire and scholars to study.

CHAPTER 7

The Restoration Story

The Silver Hill facility of the National Air and Space Museum is a unique combination.* It is a warehouse, with more than 40,000 items of air and space interest, including some 170 aircraft; it is a museum, where the hard core buffs come to feast their eyes upon planes they thought they might never see; it is an industrial facility, where some of the finest restoration work in the country is done; and it is a storehouse of aeronautical crafts and skills, embodied in the 32 people who work there.

These people, almost all craftsmen, are the heart of Silver Hill and it is their insatiable interest in the collection, their pride in their work, and their industry that makes Silver Hill a fascinating place to see. The age of the workers ranges from 20 to 60; experience ranges from twenty-year veterans of the Air Force to brand new airframe and engine mechanics, selected for their skill and their perseverance at asking for a job. Some of the individuals are master craftsmen in an amazing variety of skills: woodworking, metalworking, fabricworking, painting, engine repair, airframe repair, tool building, jig building, plastic forming, fiberglassing and so on. And perhaps most interesting of all, when they work on an aircraft, they work on it with the techniques of the period of the aircraft they are restoring. For example, if the airplane being restored is an Albatros D.Va from World War One, the craftsmen will use the same methods their German counterparts did 60 years ago: if it is a 1941 Macchi MC. 202, they then use the techniques of the Italian workers of the time.

But are they independent! And do they have opinions? And do they voice them? Yes, for they feel strongly about their work. And in a place that has perhaps 100 aircraft that need restoration, it is difficult to reach a consensus about what should be restored next. However, when the word came down that the Messerschmitt Me 262 was going to be restored so that it could be exhibited in the new Gallery of Jet Aviation, there was unamimous approval.

The only difficulty was selecting who was going to work on the aircraft. In the end, it was decided to rotate the work as it proceeded, so that as many of the craftsmen as possible would be able to have a hand in it.

The Me 262 presented some real problems, particularly in the area of corrosion

* In 1980 Silver Hill was re-named as the Paul E. Garber Facility.

When the former FE 4012 was no longer needed it went to a now defunct aviation school at the Burbank Airport, before being acquired by Ed Maloney of the Planes of Fame Museum. This photo was taken at the Museum's old Claremont California location. (Author's Photo)

control. Towards the end of the war the Germans were satisfied if an aircraft would last for 30 days, much less 30 years, and their concern with producing quantities of aircraft limited their interest in corrosion control methods. Much of the Me 262 is built of aluminum and steel; at best the preventive measure against corrosion was a light coat of paint. Due to a variety of circumstances, the aircraft spent many years in unprotected storage, where moisture could creep into the structure and where all forms of corrosion, particularly electrolytic corrosion, could take place.

The captured *Schwalbe* had been repainted several times over the years, and most of its original markings were obscured beneath layers of American paint. The paint was obviously not standard to the *Luftwaffe*, nor were the spurious cross and swastika markings. During the process, the work number of the aircraft was lost, although somewhere in the archives there must be a paper which connects the FE number used by the Army Air Force for test purposes and the original Messerschmitt factory number.

Because of the enthusiasm, even affection, for the project, it was important that standard Silver Hill procedures be adhered to. Curator of Aircraft Robert Mikesh

77

made up his usual detailed curatorial package, which indicated the degree of work to be accomplished and the markings that the aircraft would be displayed in. Several of the senior craftsmen, including the Chief of the Facility, Ed Chalkley, the Chief of the Restoration Division, Walter Roderick, and the old pro, master craftsman Joe Fichera, examined the *Schwalbe* to determine exactly how the work would be approached.

Everyone knew that corrosion control would be the most challenging task, and they were to be more correct than they knew. Uncovering the original markings, including not only the national and squadron markings, but the standard "No Steps" and other stenciled information of war planes, was of critical importance.

A real fan of the aircraft, Mike Lyons, undertook to hand sand carefully every area where original German markings could be found. It was an enormously tedious task, and a delicate one, for Mike had to sand off the American paint, but leave the first

The museum's FE 111 fitted with FE 4012's "Recce" nose.

coat of German paint unharmed. Many hours of fine wet sanding later, the aircraft was dappled, the German markings showing faintly beneath the multiple layers of peacetime paint.

Mike next used pounce paper, a lightweight, translucent material not unlike silkspan, which was placed over the individual markings. The position of the marking would be carefully identified by reference to rivets, section lines, panels, etc., and then copied carefully onto the pounce paper. When every marking had been recorded, Mike filed the papers away for later use.

Mike's detective work was invaluable in determining the original camouflage colors and markings which were to be later duplicated.

These then were two major decisions: to convert the aircraft back to its most probable original configuration, that of a standard Messerschmitt Me 262A-1a fighter, and to apply Mike's hard-won discoveries on the exact markings and patterns used when the aircraft was in combat.

Joe Fichera, a smiling, gray-haired veteran who is only happy when he is working on airplanes, compiled a massive 45 page single spaced typewritten report on what needed to be done. The report is broken down into 12 sections, detailing what each subassembly of the aircraft needed, and including an analysis of the missing parts, material required and estimated manhours to restore. It is worthwhile to excerpt a section of Joe's report just to show the depth of detail he reached. On the nose section of the aircraft, which runs from forward of the cockpit to the tip of the airplane's nose, and includes the gunbay and nose gear retraction assembly, Joe noted 29 different elements requiring attention, ranging from "several dents in nose cone around gun camera opening" to "American bolt and nut installed in nose gear linkage." Following are his comments on one of the 29 items, the nose gear:

"2. Remove nose gear as an assembly. Remove trunion bolts, disconnect strut actuating cylinders, clamp for nose and drop gear assembly out of nose section. Remove top access panels on nose section and photograph interior of nose section. (*Author's note: All restorations are photographed step by step throughout the process.*) Remove all paint on access panels with paint remover. Neutralize paint remover with warm water or high pressure water spray. Remove wooden plugs in gun openings. Remove nose section by disconnecting two top structs and two lower bolts after disconnecting hydraulic and electrical wires. Remove all camera equipment including wire bundles and quick disconnects. Do not cut wires. Go to nearest bus bar or quick disconnect to remove. Retain all equipment removed from nose for cataloguing and storage. Remove glass panel and frame on bottom right hand side and cover opening with steel using a flush type patch repair. Remove all paint on nose section including interior. Sandblast rust inside with glassbeads. Prime interior of nose section below camera shelf. Cover camera hole with sheet steel cut to fit hole and tack weld in place about every six inches around circumference. Weld plate between tack welds to prevent buckling. Also leave approximately ⅛" gap between plates for expansion while welding. After welding plates in grind welds down to match area and mount gun mounts in place as needed. Provide openings and attachments for shell chutes and related equipment if available. Remove blisters from access doors and fill in hole with sheet steel .080, weld in similar to nose shelf repair. Grind weld down flush with surrounding area. Local manufacture hat sections out of .065 steel and form to contour of doors, spot weld in place spacing welds same distance apart as original welds. Repair door latches sandblast mechanism and phosphate after repairs. Prime nose access doors with zinc chromate inside and outside. Fill in screw holes where blisters attached with body filler and sand down smooth to surrounding area. Apply several coats of primer surfacer to exterior of doors and wet sand. Paint colors specified in curatorial package after assembly to main fuselage. Apply pinked edge tape to seam and round patches over bolt holes. Apply several coats of dope on fabric then spray with primer surfacer and paint."

That is just half of one page from Joe's instructions, which are valuable not so much as a guide for the men doing the restoration, who are so knowledgeable that they could do without it, but as a resource for anyone doing a similar restoration in the future.

Fichera's analysis of missing parts and equipment is also important, for it permitted Bob Mikesh to get started on his endless rounds of finding out where the parts could be located or if that was not possible, where parts or drawings were located so that duplicates could be made up. This work could go on concurrently with the restoration in most cases, but had to be concluded by the time the aircraft was ready for assembly. Some of the missing items could be made up from the National Air and Space Museum's collection of instruments, radios and armament. Others had to be sought out from museums owning Me 262s. The gun mounts, for example, were missing. They had originally been made of forged steel and would have required hundreds of manhours to reproduce from scratch. Ed Maloney of Planes of Fame Museum in California, generously agreed to sell these items from his own Me 262, the former FE 4012.

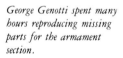

George Genotti spent many hours reproducing missing parts for the armament section.

The I beam stands save many manhours effort, for two persons can push either fuselage or wing assembly to any point in the shop.

Surprisingly, the materials costs for a restoration like this are relatively low; only $1,481.66. The principal cost is in labor. Joe had estimated 4,630 manhours, recognizing that he could not tell how much corrosion control work would be necessary. As it turned out, the corrosion was far more extensive than had been expected (it almost always is) and the extra work required for the wings ran the total restoration manhours required up to 6,077.

The number of manhours is a very poor way to record the ingenuity, effort and even love that went into the restoration. In the abstract, the concept of restoring a historic World War II fighter is one that excites almost every aviation buff. The reality of spending hundreds of hours sanding, drilling, riveting, washing, masking and painting the aircraft is quite another thing, and it is a tribute to the morale of the men who worked on the airplane that no one avoided any job, no matter how tedious or unpleasant; things were accepted as they were, and the work was pursued in the businesslike manner that characterizes the Silver Hill facility.

After Joe made his study, which included quite a bit of disassembly, the airplane was completely disassembled into its component parts. One labor-saving technique that the Silver Hill crew uses is to create portable dollies for each major construction element. These are made up of six inch I beams, and mounted on large castering wheels. They are custom tailored to the individual aircraft so that the wing, fuselage, empennage, etc., can all be moved around from position to position without difficulty and without damage. The stands take about five working days to build, but save far more time than that during the restoration process.

Work proceeds on each disassembled section concurrently, just as it does on a regular aircraft assembly line. The one "choke point" is the requirement for corrosion control treatment of the thousands of smaller parts, fasteners, springs, oleo assemblies, etc., which have to be scheduled through Will Powell's "laboratory" where precisely the right process is used to clean, etch, or even plate. Will was an experienced pilot and mechanic when he took over the corrosion control work several years ago; by lots of study and a tremendous amount of practice, he has trained himself to be an expert in the field. He schedules the thousands of parts from as many as five or six different ongoing projects, gets them out on time, and he and his assistant, Bayne Rector, never lose one.

Let us examine the aircraft, component by component, to see how the restoration work was done.

The single most important task is corrosion control. Will Powell runs the complex corrosion control lab as a computer would.

82

Fuselage

The fuselage was disassembled into four major sections: the nose cone, the main fuselage, the cockpit "bathtub" and the tail cone.

Mike Lyons continued his work on the fuselage, joined by George Genotti, who had serviced the B-17s that the Me 262 was designed to shoot down. George is a sturdy, intelligent, tenacious man who can fix *anything* and whose write-ups contributed greatly to this book. The principal task on the nose section was to convert it from the reconnaissance nose back to its original fighter condition. This involved removing the large teardrop shaped blisters, whose only purpose had been to streamline the bulge of the big cameras. The removal of the blisters left a gaping hole in the gun bay doors which had to be filled to match the existing structure as closely as possible.

When the aircraft was built, the stringers and ribs which reinforced the .080 steel skin of the nose section were mass produced. At Silver Hill, small male and female dies had to be made to reproduce these items. Once the dies were made, the sections could be formed and the nose repaired, *after* a lot of hand fitting and adroit use of a leather mallet.

Aircraft subassemblies are unwieldy to handle, for there are usually no pick-up points and the center of gravity is not defined. The fuselage broke down into four major sections.

The only way to remove corrosion from the major fuselage section was to "tent" it and then crawl inside. Mike Lyons spent almost 100 miserable hours burling the inside with walnut shells.

The results were worth the effort. This shows the fuselage aft of the rear fuel tanks.

The major fuselage section was corroded, and too large to be placed in any of the chemical corrosion control vats in Will Powell's shop. As an alternative, the openings in the fuselage were sealed with a plastic tent and masking tape, and Mike Lyons crawled inside fitted out with a respirator apparatus and a blasting gun for spraying ground walnut shells. After ten days of this tedious, choking task, the fuselage interior looked freshly minted.

The Fuhrerraum (cockpit) was a major subassembly and illustrates the ingenious subcontracting process used by the Germans to disperse their industry.

OPPOSITE PAGE:

The refurbished cockpit was complete down to decals.

Dale Bucy laboriously removed corroded steel skin sections and replaced them with hand formed duplicates, a time-consuming, difficult task. All unpainted surfaces were then coated with water-white, a clear preservative.

All necessary repairs had been made prior to the application of the water-white; the interior fittings were restored, and the fuselage was ready for reassembly, after the cockpit was reinstalled and the exterior surface prepared.

The exterior of the fuselage was easier to handle, with conventional techniques being used to remove the finish, check corrosion, make repairs and prepare for reassembly.

The cockpit "bathtub" was an example of German production ingenuity at its best. It was called the *"Fuhrerraum"* and was completely separate from the aircraft. Easy to install, the self-contained unit had the instrument panel, electrical consoles, stick and rudder, throttles, seat, battery and every component of the cockpit assembled as a unit, ready to plug into the fuselage. Curator Mikesh had indicated that the finish was to be "restored to near new condition as opposed to having an operationally used appearance." Mike Lyons put in hundreds of hours bringing every detail back to life, from the basic flight instruments down to replacing the timeworn original German decals with identical ones made in-house by John Siske.

The empennage section was given the same treatment as the fuselage. Some control fixtures such as the rudder actuating rods and bell crank, and the elevator actuating rods had to be manufactured, since they were, inexplicably, missing.

86

Fig. 1. INSTRUMENT PANEL--Me 262 COCKPIT

1. Airspeed indicator	6. Ammunition counter switch	11. Cockpit heat control	16. Hydraulic pressure
2. Flight indicator	7. Tachometers	12. Fuel counters	17. Nose wheel brake
3. Rate of climb indicator	8. Tailpipe gas temperature indicators	13. Free air temp. bulb selector	18. Ventilator control
4. Altimeter	9. Fuel injection press. gauges	14. Photo-observer switch	
5. Radio compass	10. Fuel gauges	15. Free air temp. gauge	

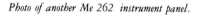

Photo of another Me 262 instrument panel.

Test aircraft often had American instruments substituted. Note changes in actimeter, fuel counters, etc. (Courtesy of Richard Seeley)

Fig. 2 LEFT-HAND SIDE FORWARD--Me 262 COCKPIT

1. Operating handle--emergency landing gear system	4. Horizontal stabilizer trim indicator	9. Throttle controls
2. Operating handle--emergency flap lowering system	5. Position indicator--left main gear	10. Fuel shut-off & selector valve
3. Horizontal stabilizer trim control lever	6. Position indicator--nose gear	11. Rudder trim control
	7. Position indicator--right main gear	12. Rudder trim tab position indic.
	8. Breathing oxygen control valve	13. Breathing oxygen indicator and flowmeter

Fig. 3. LEFT-HAND SIDE--Me 262 COCKPIT

1. Circuit-breaker	5. Position indicator--left main gear
2. Flap control push-buttons	6. Position indicator--nose gear
3. Landing gear control push-buttons	7. Position indicator--right main gear
4. Compressed air pressure gauge	

Further cockpit details. (Courtesy of Richard Seeley)

Fig. 4. RIGHT-HAND SIDE--Me 262 COCKPIT

1. Canopy release lever	9. Stabilizer control switch	17. Radio control box--BC-602-A
2. Fuel transfer pumps switch	10. Inverter switch	18. L.H. Riedel starter switch
3. Fuel pump switch	11. L.H. generator switch	19. R.H. Riedel starter switch
4. Fuel pump switch	12. R.H. generator switch	20. L.H. tachometer range button
5. Radio switch--Fu G 16	13. Battery switch	21. R.H. tachometer range button
6. Radio switch--Fu G 25a	14. Bomb release handle	22. Earphone volume control
7. Recognition lights switch	15. L.H. fuel manifold drain	23. Windshield heater switch
8. Pitot heat switch	16. R.H. fuel manifold drain	24. Flare release switch

Mike's sanding brought out
the original German
markings which had been
overpainted and clumsily
reproduced.

The Wings

The wings, mounted on one of Silver Hill's typical portable dollies, turned out to be a corrosion disaster area. The ailerons, landing gear, flaps and slats were all removed, and the exterior of the wing given the usual paint removal and corrosion control treatment. Because of the extensive use of steel in the aircraft, the restorers were apprehensive that parts of the wing not visible through the many access plates might be rusted. A little experimentation proved they were correct, and expert metal workers Bill Stevenson and Bob Padgett launched into one of the most extensive corrosion control efforts ever undertaken by the Museum.

The wing had been mounted upright on the stand, and an analysis was made of how to approach the problem of disassembling the permanently installed thick skin sections without losing the alignment of the wing. If the wing was entirely disassembled, it would be necessary to virtually recreate the original Messerschmitt jigs to get it back together. The thought of this was frightening, not only because of the immense number of man-hours involved, but because it might have proven to be impossible to obtain the same manufacturing tolerances that the original jigs provided.

As an alternative, Stevenson and Padgett decided to remove alternate panels and to fabricate fixtures which would support the weakened structure and prevent misalignment.

To start, 12 aluminum panels, each approximately 13 x 17 inches, were removed

Above, the first operational jet fighter shown next to its stablemate, a Messerschmitt 410.

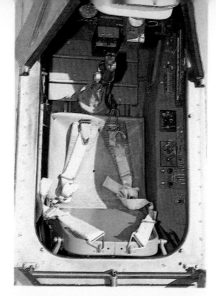

The restoration process at the Paul E. Garber Facility involved more than 6,000 hours of meticulous, loving craftsmanship.

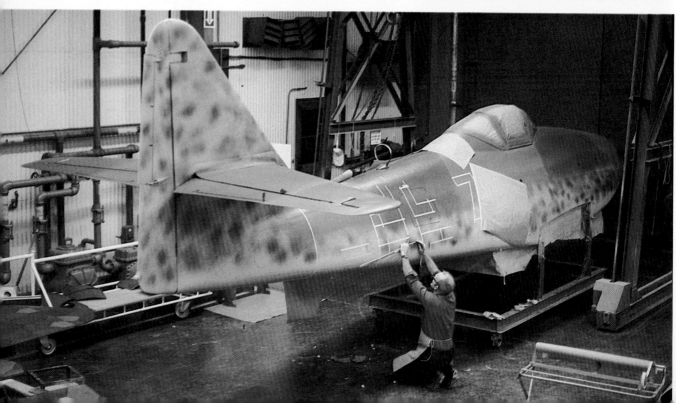

The wings were much more badly corroded than had been anticipated. (Mike Lyons Photo)

Bob Padgett and Bill Stevenson removed and replaced every panel on the wing to route out all traces of corrosion.

The exterior surface of the wing was sanded and treated for corrosion.

from the bottom of the wing. They were cleaned, etched, and painted, as was the interior of the wing. The panels were reapplied to the wing with the temporary fasteners, using the original rivet holes for alignment. Holes were countersunk to accept the fasteners.

Next six large inboard panels, approximately 24" x 24" in size were removed from the wing by drilling out more tahan 1,200 rivets. The usual paint stripping, etching and corrosion control treatment were applied.

The steel spar was found to be rusted and all steel interior parts were treated by abrasive blasting with glass bead material to remove rust. (The problem of then removing the glass bead dust was almost as tedious and time consuming as the rust removal itself.) As in every case where the manufacturer left a surface unpainted, the interior was then coated with a clear water-white material for protection.

The surface was filled with body putty and sanded again.

Mirror smooth, the wing was primed.

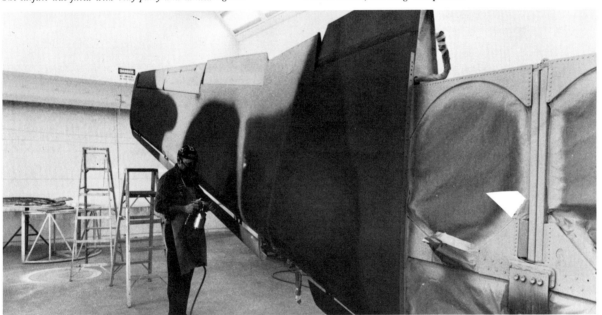

Charley Parmely applied the camouflage in the same patterns found on the aircraft.

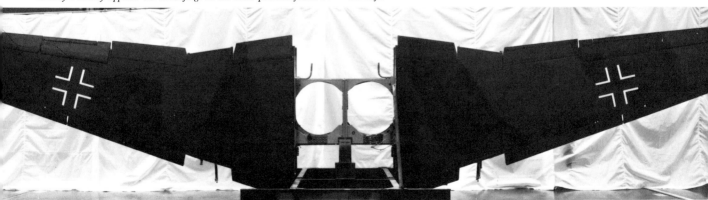

The finished wing, ready for assembly.

The fuselage went through a similar process. The nose section was doubly difficult, because of the extensive corrosion due to the German mixed use of steel and aluminum, and because the "incorrect" reconnaissance nose had to be modified back to a standard fighter nose.

The panels were then reinstalled with temporary fasteners, to give rigidity to the wing. The original rivet holes were located, and the re-riveting began. Because of the various processes, including annealing the rivets, it took six hours of work to do each panel. Where the rivets had to attach to the main spar, a high speed reamer, cooled with lubricating oil, was used in place of the conventional drill bits.

During the whole process of restoring the wing, special tools had to be fabricated. Harvey Napier, perhaps the best machinist in the aircraft restoration business, formed special bucking bars for riveting in closed areas, modified conventional rivet squeezers to fit the odd size rivets being used, and in general made an impossible task possible.

When the final panel had been put in place, all other units including slats, ailerons, landing gear and so on were installed, and the wing was ready for finishing.

The engine was torn down, refurbished, all corrosion arrested, and then built up again. This was Bill Reese's first important assignment at Silver Hill, and he went all out to do a first rate job.

Engines

The Junkers Jumo 004B engines were found to be in relatively good condition, with only mild corrosion and a few dented parts. Because the engines on the Messerschmitt Me 262 were changed so frequently, and because parts of the engines were so often interchanged during maintenance and rebuilding, it was decided to save time by combining parts of three engines to create the two which would be installed. The engines were completely disassembled, cleaned and repaired, and corrosion control materials applied. Exterior painting was done as required to recreate the appearance of a new engine, and the engines were reinstalled. One of Silver Hill's newest employees, Bill Reese, worked with Bob Padgett to do the engine job. It was a formidable task for a new man, but the finished product passed muster with his master craftsman associates.

Dale Bucy used the right engine cowling as a guide to hand form the missing parts on the left nacelle, a difficult job with many compound curves.

The engine, on its special dolly ready for installation.

This piece of nacelle cowling from the left engine was missing from the aircraft. To recreate it Dale Bucy photographed the existing piece on the right engine, reversed the negative, blew the print up and made a pattern.

Other Components

The armament bay had to be completely reconstructed, and working from borrowed parts, drawings, photos and good common sense, George Genotti recreated the structures which supported the four 30 mm cannon.

The canopy had discolored badly during its years of storage but it was carefully buffed to a serviceable condition.

The tires and wheels were also in bad shape. The wheels had some magnesium elements which were badly corroded, and the tires were of course flat and misshapen. The wheels were completely repaired, which involved the forming of some new parts, and the tires were given a long soaking in a patented product, Armor-all. They softened up enough to be mounted back on the wheels and inflated, and look today almost as good as when they left the factory.

Carroll Dorsey did a fine job refinishing the wooden R4M rocket racks, and he and Larry Motz spent hours disassembling components.

Finishing Techniques

The secret of finishing a restored aircraft lies in its preparation. The airplane was finished by major components, assembled, and then detail markings and clean-up work done.

While different sections required some differences in technique, the fuselage will serve as a good example of how the work was done.

All paint was first removed with a paint remover, followed by a long neutralizing bath with hot water. When dry, the fuselage was washed by hand with a special solvent to clean the skin, rivet heads and seams. The interior of the fuselage was treated for corrosion removal. All the aluminum was treated with a special aluminum cleaner, washed, etched, and deoxidized. Areas to be painted were treated with Chromicoat L-25 before painting.

Any German markings that appeared on the inside of the fuselage were preserved with a coat of water-white.

The exterior was then given a coat of zinc chromatic primer, followed by several coats of primer surfacer. The sanding process began with wet or dry #320 sandpaper. All low spots, dents and creases were filled with body filler, and wet sanded to match.

Next, all seams were covered with 2" pinked tape doped on the seam. Several coats of dope were given to fill, being sanded lightly after every second coat. The taped surfaces were then covered with primer surfacer.

The fuselage was assembled, seams taped, and another coat of zinc chromate primer, followed by primer surfacer, applied. The fuselage was wet sanded until smooth, and was then ready for painting as required by Mikesh's curatorial package. Master story teller, "Handsome" Charlie Parmley, carefully sprayed the aircraft, recreating its original appearance.

Markings
and Camouflage

Mike Lyons had laboriously uncovered the exact camouflage demarcation lines, so the original paint scheme was known. They generally followed the *Luftwaffe* marking specifications for the time, with the sort of deviations you might expect in a production situation.

Paint chips were removed from all areas and were compared with Munsel cards to determine the original German colors used. Colors and corresponding German and American color codes are found in Chapter Eight.

The upper surface had a dark brownish green color over which was applied a darker green. The lower surfaces were finished in blue gray. Interestingly, the Germans had somewhat laboriously painted the blue gray under surface around the stencils, rather than applying the stencils over the blue gray. Silver Hill followed the same practice, for authenticity. Landing gear struts and wheel door interiors were finished in a green gray.

The upper surface colors were blended into the gray-white primer undersurface over a wide area, leaving no easily discernible mark.

The operational markings of the aircraft add a surprising note of color for the stage of the war in which the plane was operating. The wings and fuselage had the full size national markings of the period, including the swatstika on the rudder. The aircraft carried the insignia of *Jagdeschwader* 7, a charging white fox on a blue shield, as well as the unit's distinctive red and blue fuselage bands.

A vertical bar, painted midway between the blue and the red bands identified the plane as belonging to *III Gruppe* of JG 7. The bar's yellow color shows that it belongs to the 11th *Staffel*. As a final mark, a large yellow 7 is painted on each side of the fuselage, identifying it as the 7th plane of the 11th *Staffel*.

The pilot's victory markings were reapplied. After this there only remained the application of the dozens of maintenance instructions, octane markings, and so on with which military planes of every nation are so liberally equipped.

Suddenly, incredibly, the aircraft was finished; the thousands of hours of hard work, the endless stream of barked knuckles, the tedium of sanding, filling, resanding and refilling over. The airplane stands as it must have in Germany, looking capable, powerful, ready for combat. The men who worked on it so long did not stare at it; they looked at it indirectly, proud of what they had done, conscious of the fact that they have created a tangible bit of history. As long as the Museum lasts, their work will be on exhibit, a testimony to their patience and their skills.

A proud group with a proud airplane. From left, Bill Reese, Mike Lyons, Dale Bucy, Charlie Parmley, George Genotti and Bob Padgett.

Technical Description

The technical description of the Messerschmitt Me 262 is fascinating, for it combines a number of amazing elements. Here is an aircraft built for speeds beyond any other aircraft's capability, but which must be assembled by less than skilled laborers under primitive conditions, from materials of inferior quality. Here is the most advanced airframe in the world, being built in forest clearings, with minimum wind tunnel tests, and deliberately designed so that tolerances do not have to be exact. Here are the first jet engines to go into mass production, compromised from the start by lack of strategic materials and the need for rapid assembly, able to burn low grade fuel, good for perhaps ten to 25 hours of running time at the maximum, and yet capable of carrying fighter pilots faster than any piston engine plane would ever fly.

The success of the Messerschmitt effort was possible because of the pedigreed background of the firm's former products, because of the Messerschmitt philosophy of giving engineers their head, and because of the primal joy that the group felt to be working on something that was clearly a revolutionary step forward.

The success of the Me 262 was also due in part to the enormous experience the firm had gained in the years since 1933, when demand for Bf 109 fighters had gone up, up and up and the firm had produced or studied no less than 30 different types. Just as certain designers can impress their personalities on the external appearances of planes, as Sir Sidney Camm imparted his characteristic signature to Hawker fighters, or Geoffrey de Havilland gave a characteristic shape to de Havilland designs, so do engineers tend to use past experience in their creation of new designs. It is no surprise then that so many features found in the Me 262 were derived from previous practice on the Bf 109, Bf 110, and Me 210 and 410 aircraft.

General Overview

The Messerschmitt Me 262 combined in one package the most advanced engines, the most advanced airframe and the heaviest armament package yet seen in a fighter. An all metal, low wing, cantilever monoplane, the *Schwalbe* was built with simple aluminum alloys, and steel; the general fit of the aluminum skin was rough, a problem Messerschmitt aerodynamicists solved with plenty of tape and body putty for seams.

The 18½ degree sweep of the Me 262s's wing was intended to offset some center of gravity problems. It also fortuitously delayed the onset of compressibility and permitted the Me 262 the exceptionally high limiting Mach number of .86. (The postwar Republic P-84C "Thundejet" had a limiting Mach of only .82.)

In this close-up one can note the slats deployed on the left wing. Pilot is Major Russ Schleeh, U.S.A.A.F..

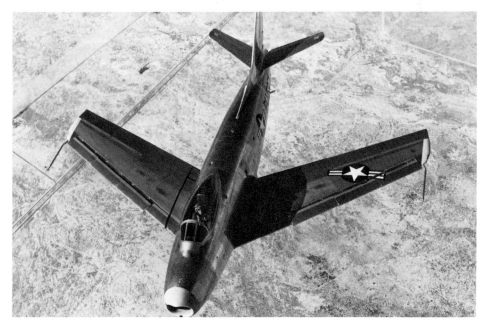

The F-86's Sabre's wings had greater sweep but were equipped with essentially similar slots.

All difficult forming was done in the quenched condition, and much jigging was avoided by the use of self aligning bushings rather than precisely fitted nuts and bolts.

The whole aircraft shows a remarkable adaptability for sub-component production at diverse locations, being designed for relatively simple assembly at the primitive forest and cave factories to which the Reich was reduced in its last months. Weight control was evidently not as much a concern as production ease; the same airplane, designed to American standards might have been as much as 500 to 1,000 pounds lighter, but it would have been correspondingly more difficult to build. German production experts tried to reduce the number of manhours required to build the Me 262 to 6,000; in actual practice, it required about twice that.

Construction Details The wing of the Me 262, with its sweepback, slots and underslung nacelles, must surely be considered to be its most advanced feature, one that proved to be influential in the design of jet aircraft for years. The aircraft was originally intended to have a straight wing, with relatively small diameter jet engines routed through the main spar. As previously discussed, the ever changing type and size of engines rendered this impractical, and the decision was made to go to underslung nacelles, still with a straight wing. An increase in engine size and weight upset center of gravity calculations, so that the outer panels of the wings were swept back from engine nacelles to maintain the center of gravity. Later, airflow problems dictated that the wing center sections be thickened, and to maintain the same aerodynamic thickness, the chord of the center section was increased by extending the sweep of the wing in a straight line from the fuselage all the way to the tip. At the same time, slots were placed inboard, and there was an enormous improvement both in lift, reportedly as much as 30%, and in the flying qualities.[1]

The 18 and ½° degree sweepback of the wing was moderate by today's standards, but revolutionary for the time, and gave the plane an arrow shape that was absolutely distinctive. The sweep was found to have the important incidental advantage of delaying compressibility, and raising the critical Mach number to 0.86.

While the Germans were familiar with the laminar flow wings of captured P-51 Mustangs, they did not have the skilled laborers or the time to create the manufacturing standards necessary to produce a laminar flow wing. It so happened that the use of slots, which were necessary to cure the very bad boundary layer condition at the tips of the wings at the stall, mitigated against the use of a laminar flow airfoil anyway—in short, sweepback required slots and slots required a normal airfoil section, especially given the German quality control standards of the time.

Even though early technical documents describe the Me 262 wing as being single spar, it is actually a two spar wing, with a very small channel section rear spar. The main spar is an I beam which tapers from about 14 inches at the aircraft center line to three inches at the point where the wing tip attached.[2] The spar is made up primarily of chrome molybdenum steel, with aluminum webs, and is located at the point of maximum thickness in the wings, about 40% of the chord. The entire structure creates a torsion box, except for the space aft of the main spar which houses the retracted landing gear strut, and with its heavy aluminum skin it was able to withstand great loads and was relatively easy to manufacture. The aluminum skin

1. "Evaluation of the Me 262", project No. NAD-29, by Roy W. Adams, February 1947.

was not anodized. Early models were painted for corrosion control but even this was eliminated later in the war.

The wing is made in two halves which were joined together before fuselage assembly. The rear spar caps are connected by two steel plates, one above and one below. The main landing gear wheels retract into the central space between the two spars. The wing rib here is of steel and has doubler plates and reinforcements either riveted or spot welded as necessary. It acts as a beam to transfer the vertical shears of the spars into the fuselage, and all the torsion in the wing into the two spars as vertical shears.

The wing is attached to the fuselage by means of the heavy ribs mentioned previously; a 20 mm diameter bolt in single shear at the forward end is very accurately fitted and is the key for positioning the wing. A similar bolt near the rear spar has a looser fit, reflecting the German design philosophy of trading accuracy for ease of assembly.

The slats are made of steel sheet of .040 inch thickness, for strength and rigidity, and they run on tracks. The slats are in three sections on each wing, with the two outboard sections being pinned together. There is no synchronization with the inner wing slat. The slats would begin to open at about 186 mph in a glide and 279 mph in a climb.

Each aileron is made in two pieces for installation purposes, with each half slipped over a hinge at its far end and then the other hinge bolted in via an access door in the top surface. Self aligning ball bearing hinges acted as connecting points for the two sections also. There is a ground adjustable tab for trim.

The all metal flaps extend in two sections, one on each side of the nacelle; they run on completely internal tracks, and operate by one hydraulic cylinder in the right wing which drove them via a system of bell cranks and push rods.

Altogether, the impression of the wing construction is one of elegant simplicity; there seems to be an absolute minimum of structure, yet all components are of adequate size; some indeed seem to be oversize, because simplicity of manufacture came before weight control.

The Fuselage

The semi-monocoque fuselage is divided into five sub-assemblies, consisting of the nose cone, armament and nose wheel section, forward fuel tank and cockpit section, rear fuel tanks, and radio section and empennage section.

The nose cone is a spun part attached with screws. The gun section is composed of a box structure housing the retracted nose wheel; the guns are located above this, and strength is provided in a primitive but effective manner by two steel tie tubes. Four bolts hold this section to the next part of the fuselage.

The cockpit section resembles nothing so much as a bathtub. Boxed in fore and aft by 198 gallon fuel tanks, it was completely fitted out with controls, instruments, seat, and so on. It was attached to the fuselage by two solid web aluminum alloy bulkheads, and the structure was shaped around three hoop frames and one channel

The fuselage was of semi-monocoque construction. The "checks" which appear here are the seams which had been taped and filled, but not overpainted.

former. It was obviously designed to be suitable for pressurization which would have undoubtedly been incorporated in later production runs.

The fuselage sections containing the tanks and the cockpit have no frames except at the attachment points. At a circumferential skin joint, one sheet is formed in such a way as to mate with the next section. The self sealing tanks are inserted from the bottom, supported by a moulded plywood panel over the tank; studs are molded into the tank top and sides for attachment to the plywood, which is in turn bolted to the fuselage structure.

The empennage section is conventional, attached to the rest of the fuselage with multiple tension bolts. The vertical fin is integral with the tail section.

No longerons were used in the fuselage construction; instead fuselage stringers are heavy gage hat sections, placed, at the maximum, 12 inches apart.

One is struck by how hollow the Me 262 fuselage is compared to later aircraft; from the aft fuel tank aft there are just a few components; even forward there seems to be plenty of room compared to a modern fighter.

The canopy on production aircraft was a clear vision blown type, not so elegant as the Mustang's, but still providing an amazing field of view, particularly forward and down.

Experimentation was going on with ejection seats, and had Me 262 production continued, one would certainly have been fitted.

The cockpit was sandwiched by fuel tanks, and placed directly above the one piece wing.

The armament package in the nose was very heavy, consisting of four 30 mm MK 108 cannon, with 100 rounds per gun for the upper two guns and 80 rounds per gun for the lower two. Various armament packages had been devised for the aircraft, including as many as six cannon in the nose. Some special purpose versions had fewer guns.

Besides the 198 Imperial gallon main fuel tanks which sandwiched the cockpit area, there were two smaller tanks. One, of 132 Imperial gallons, was just behind the aft main tank, while the other, of 37.4 Imperial gallon capacity was below the cockpit area. The pilot had to manage the fuel so that the aft tank was emptied before entering into any prolonged, high speed dives, otherwise the aircraft could pitch up violently upon pull-up.

Engines

Anselm Franz's Junkers Jumo 004B-1 axial flow jet engine was a large power plant, 152 inches long from the intake to the tip of the exhaust, 30 inches in diameter at its widest part. It weighed 750 kg (1650 lbs), turned 8,700 rpm, operated at 775°C and provided 2,000 pounds of thrust.

The forward nose cowling is double-skinned, holding an annular gasoline tank which supplies fuel both to the amazing engine starter, and also to the combustion chamber, for starting.

Inside the circular nose cowling is a familiar looking spinner housing the two cylinder, two cycle Reidel horizontally opposed gasoline engine which develops 10 horsepower at 6,000 rpm. It is much like a little outboard motor, even to the point of having a pull type cable for emergency use. Normal start was electrical.

Immediately behind the starter is the gear casing which is used to drive the engine accessories, and behind this is the compressor. This consists of a 220 pound rotor section, and a stator casting, which, with blades, weighs 200 pounds. The eight stage compressor has an amazing variety of types of materials and finishes, ranging from stamped aluminum to a zinc coated sheet steel. Even within a single engine variations were found in the materials and method of assembly of stator blades.

The backbone of the 004 was a complex aluminum casting which provided the engine attachment points, supported the compressor case, the combustion chamber

The Junker Jumo 004 engines were enclosed in the sleek undersluing nacelles. The pointed cone at the rear of the engine is the "zweibel" (onion) which was used to vary the exhaust area to suit the engine speed.

Positioning the engines under the wing had a number of advantages. They were easy to service or change, and larger engines could have been fitted without extensive redesign. They were, however, vulnerable to the ingestion of foreign objects. The cone shaped fairing centered in the engine intake houses the Reidel starter.

assembly, the turbine nozzle, turbine bearings, and finally, the entire exhaust system.

Each of the six combustion chambers was built up of three major components—a mild steel outer casing, the flame tube, and a corrugated aluminized steel liner which ducted cooling air through the outer casing. Starting plugs are provided in three of the six chambers.

Hot gas was ducted from the combustion chambers to the 61 blade turbine wheel. The turbine wheel had been intended from the beginning to have hollow air cooled blades, but the pressure of time had dictated that the first versions have solid turbine blades. The blade was formed from conically rolled sheetmetal by folding it and welding at the trailing edge. The material used, "Cromadur," required no precious nickel, was easier to produce, and was more reliable in operation.

Aft of the turbine was the exhaust cone, made up of two fairings composed of aluminized mild steel. The double skinned outer fairing allowed compressor air to flow between the skins for cooling.

The inner fairing houses a rack gear which moves a bullet (Onion or Zwiebel to the Germans) which had the effect of reducing the exit area between 20 and 25%. The bullet was set in the retracted position for starting to give greater exhaust area and prevent overheating, and then moved aft to decrease the area to give greater

114

The horizontal stabilizer incidence could be adjusted electrically. This feature was adopted by many later aircraft. (U.S. Air Force)

velocity for take-off and in flight. It had to be continuously adjusted manually (although it had been originally intended to have an automatic regulator) and was certainly a bother to the pilot. It was also a hazard, for if it failed and blew back to the exhaust outlet, it could seal it off, causing immediate flame out. The resulting asymmetric forces slewed the plane sideways, blanking the empennage and often causing a fatal dive.

Although the engine was started on gasoline, it burned the noxious smelling German J-2 fuel, which was derived from brown coal.

In light of some recent air accidents, it is interesting to note that the engine was suspended by three points, two at the leading edge of the wing and one just aft of the main spar. One of the forward connections and the aft connection had fore and aft play; the other connection had lateral play and was designed to carry all of the thrust load.

The Empennage

The all metal tail surfaces were characterized by their clean shape, ample size, and obviously well thought out production simplicity. The elevators were mounted high on the vertical stabilizer, and were mass balanced, with ground adjustable trim tabs, usually riveted in place. Trim was accomplished by adjusting the incidence of the entire stabilizer by means of an electric motor driven screw jack, which could be actuated from the cockpit.

The rudder was also mass balanced, a design throwback for a jet aircraft, but an easy solution to some flutter problems. The rudder was very effective, able to damp out yaw easily in the aircraft even at high speeds, and more than adequate to maintain single engine control. At 450 km/hr. (270 mph), satisfactory control was maintained with only three degrees of rudder trim.

The Undercarriage

The tricycle gear of the Messerschmitt 262 was regarded as a real innovation by the Germans, even though numerous aircraft had been fitted with it by 1942. The materials used in the Schwalbe's gear were really more unusual than its configuration, for instead of the massive forgings used on almost all foreign aircraft, the 262 landing gear oleo struts were made from drawn seamless tubing. Axles, fittings, and so on were of relatively low grade steel. The resulting structure was relatively light weight and easy to produce, but not very robust, and was the major cause for aircraft being out of commission.

Systems

The Messerschmitt Me 262 was a simple aircraft, but not entirely spartan, for there were some redundant systems, and some of the intended equipment was quite sophisticated.

The Schwalbe's undercarriage was its weakest link. 34% of all accidents involved the undercarriage, usually the nose gear.

Perhaps most important, in terms of future applications, was the electrically operated stabilizer trim. A switch on the left side of the cockpit near the throttles enabled the pilot to quickly trim the aircraft by moving it forward for nose down, and aft for nose up. Limit switches on the stabilizer opened to prevent the pilot from holding the switch too long, and a selsyn transmitter linked to the stabilizer showed the actual setting. Pilot reports indicate that the stabilizer trim was used extensively.

The guns were fired simultaneously by means of a thumb switch on the control stick, and were charged by the pilot. Eight compressed air bottles of two liters capacity each were on board; this provided considerable excess air so that the charging system did not have to be serviced between missions.

The landing gear and flaps were hydraulically operated; motion picture films of takeoffs and landings show a rather elegant sequence in which the main gears extend, not quite simultaneously, lock down, and then the nose wheel extends; similarly, 'upon retraction, the main wheels come up first, followed by the nose wheel.

The hydraulic pressure was supplied by a small (18 liters per minute capacity) pump fitted to the left engine, so the undercarriage operated slowly. It was intended to fit a similar pump to the right engine later, which would have speeded up operation and provided increased dependability. The maximum permissible speed for gear extension was 500 kmph, and had to be rigidly ahhered to. The flaps were also hydraulically operated, and could not be lowered until the landing gear was fully extended, a safety precaution which inhibited the use of flaps to tighten turns.

High pressure air provided a backup system for both flaps and gear; in the case of the latter, the air operated the fairing doors, and the gear free-fell.

Prospective Innovations

Despite the gloomy news from every front, the German engineering staff had to presume that the war was going to continue and that improvements were going to be required through the 1945-46 time period. As a result, there were hundreds of experiments going on that appear, in hindsight, to have been a waste of time in view of the deteriorating war situation.

The most important of these, from the pilots' point of view, anyway, was the planned installation of a pressure cabin. This would have provided a much greater altitude capability than the operational Me 262, and was tested in the Me 262 V7, which had a canopy with a rubber seal, and air bled from the eighth stage of the compressor. The pressure ratio of 1:2 meant that a cabin altitude of 20,000 feet was maintained at a flight altitude of 40,000.

Second most important, perhaps, was the planned installation of an ejection seat. Seats of the period were very primitive, of course, ranging from the pneumatic type used in the Heinkel 280, from which a German pilot named Schenk made the world's first emergency use of an ejection seat on January 13, 1943, to the cartridge type used in the Heinkel He 162 and He 219. The urgency of the war situation, however, prevented ejection seats from being installed in production aircraft.

The natural desire to increase the Me 262's range and bomb load capacity led to some rather radical attempts at solutions, involving towed bombs or fuel tanks.

In one experiment, a 1,102 pound or 2,205 pound bomb was fitted with a wooden wing and towed by a 20 foot long cylindrical tow bar. A two-wheel dolly was used for takeoff, and the bomb "flew" behind the Me 262 by means of a swivel joint attachment at the tail which permitted horizontal and vertical motion. The

The Deichselschlepp a towed bomb equipped with V-1 like wings. (Courtesy J. R. Smith)

tests were not successful, as one might have predicted, especially for the larger bomb, whose wing provided too much lift, resulting in the bomb porpoising and on one occasion forcing the pilot to bail out. Woldemar Voigt has commented that part of the problem was incorrect placement of the center of gravity.

Similar experiments were run with towed fuel tanks, with similar results.

Various attempts were made to improve the Me 262 takeoff and climb capabilities by installing either jettisonable or built-in rocket engines. The Me 262C-1a *Heimatschutzer I* (Home Protector) was a standard Me 262 fighter type, with a Walter bi-fuel rocket engine mounted in the rear of the fuselage. (This was essentially the same type of engine used in the Messerschmitt Me 163B rocket interceptors, and used the same extremely dangerous combination of fuels, *T-Stoff* and *C-Stoff*.)

The rocket boosted Me 262C-1a Heimatschutzer. Rate of climb was spectacular but reliability was poor, and normal endurance was compromised. (Courtesy J. R. Smith)

The rocket engine reduced takeoff distance to a little less than 2,000 feet, and the rate of climb was sensational, approaching 10,000 feet per minute, but the requirement for rocket fuel reduced the tankage available for jet fuel by 330 of its normal 565 Imperial gallons, and consequently reduced the range to an impractical level. The project was dropped in favor of the *Heimatschutzer II,* the Me 262C-2b, which had two radical BMW combination powerplants, the 003R. This engine consisted of the long delayed in development 003A turbojet of 1,760 pounds static thrust and a BMW 718 rocket rated at 2,700 pounds of thrust.

With these powerful but temperamental engines the Me 262 achieved formidable performance, once climbing to 25,000 feet in about 90 seconds, but the entire system was too unreliable, and was dropped.

Specifications and Performance (Typical)

Wing Span	40 Ft. 11 in.
Length	39 Ft. 9 in.
Height	12 Ft. 7 in.
Empty Weight	9,742 pounds
Gross Weight	13,250 pounds
Maximum Gross Weight	15,620 pounds
Power Plants	Two Junkers Jumo 004B 1,980 pounds static thrust each
Maximum Speed	540 mph @ 19,685 Ft. (522 mph @ 15,000 in U.S. Navy Tests)
Range	526 miles @ 19,685 Ft.
T.O. Distance (14,000 lbs.)	4,000 Ft. (Approximately)
Landing Distance (14,000 lbs.)	4,000 Ft. (Approximately)
Initial Climb Rate	3,937 fpm
Service Ceiling	38,000 Feet

The above figures are the best compilation available from a variety of sources; it must be remembered that German test methods were not so exact as those of the United States and that post war U.S. testing was usually done on aircraft that could

119

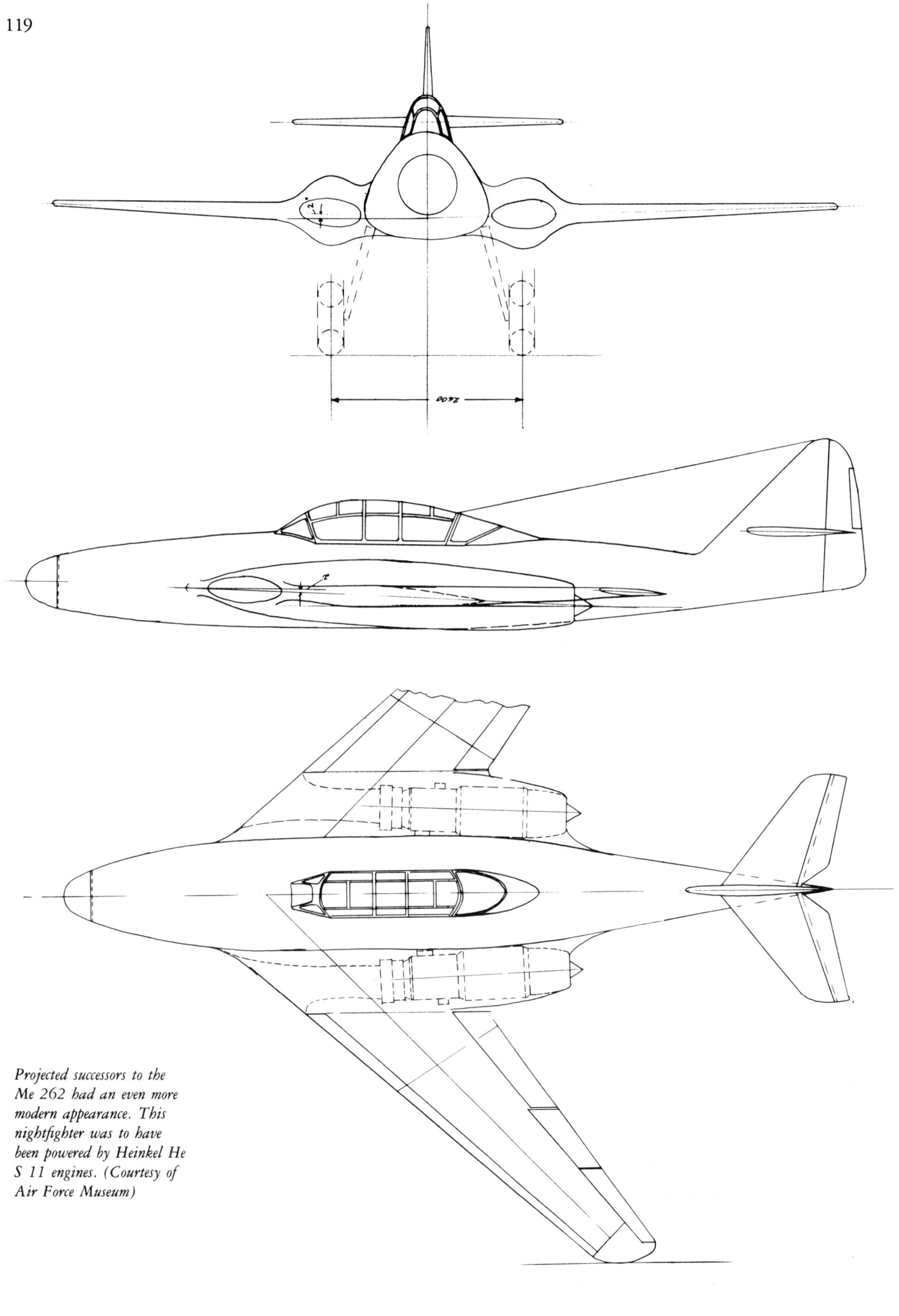

Projected successors to the Me 262 had an even more modern appearance. This nightfighter was to have been powered by Heinkel He S 11 engines. (Courtesy of Air Force Museum)

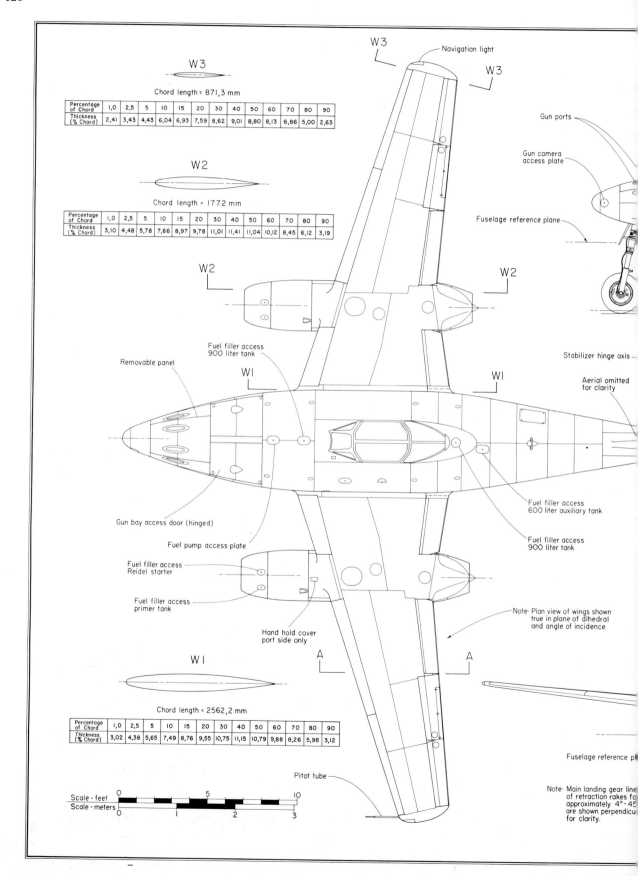

W3

Chord length = 871,3 mm

Percentage of Chord	1,0	2,5	5	10	15	20	30	40	50	60	70	80	90
Thickness (% Chord)	2,41	3,43	4,43	6,04	6,93	7,59	8,62	9,01	8,80	8,13	6,86	5,00	2,63

W2

Chord length = 1772 mm

Percentage of Chord	1,0	2,5	5	10	15	20	30	40	50	60	70	80	90
Thickness (% Chord)	3,10	4,48	5,78	7,66	8,97	9,78	11,01	11,41	11,04	10,12	8,45	6,12	3,19

W1

Chord length = 2562,2 mm

Percentage of Chord	1,0	2,5	5	10	15	20	30	40	50	60	70	80	90
Thickness (% Chord)	3,02	4,38	5,65	7,49	8,76	9,55	10,75	11,15	10,79	9,88	8,26	5,98	3,12

Navigation light

Gun ports

Gun camera access plate

Fuselage reference plane

Stabilizer hinge axis

Aerial omitted for clarity

Fuel filler access 900 liter tank

Removable panel

Gun bay access door (hinged)

Fuel pump access plate

Fuel filler access Reidel starter

Fuel filler access primer tank

Hand hold cover port side only

Fuel filler access 600 liter auxiliary tank

Fuel filler access 900 liter tank

Note: Plan view of wings shown true in plane of dihedral and angle of incidence

Pitot tube

Fuselage reference pl

Note: Main landing gear line of retraction rakes fo approximately 4°-45 are shown perpendicu for clarity.

Scale - feet
Scale - meters

121

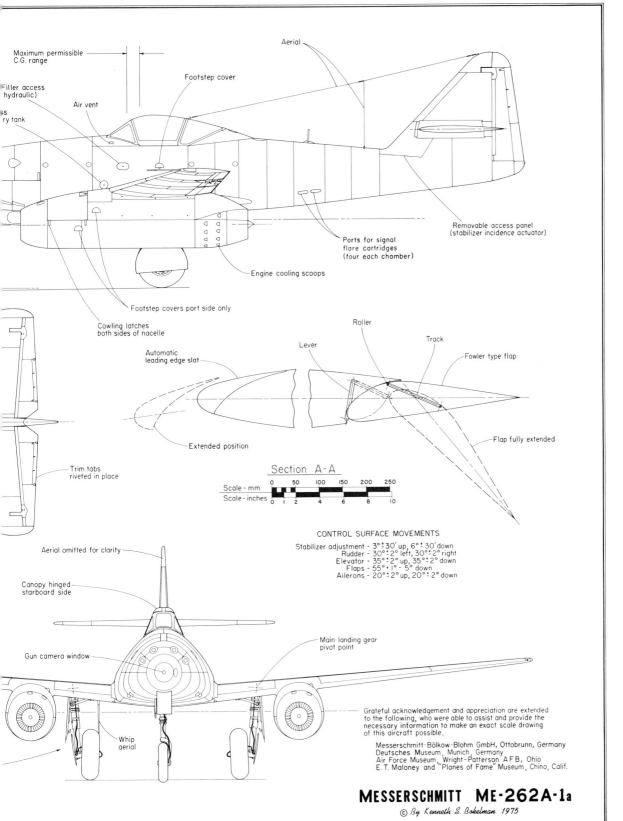

Maximum permissible
C.G. range

Aerial

Footstep cover

Filler access
hydraulic)

Air vent

ry tank

Removable access panel
(stabilizer incidence actuator)

Ports for signal
flare cartridges
(four each chamber)

Engine cooling scoops

Footstep covers port side only

Cowling latches
both sides of nacelle

Roller

Lever

Track

Fowler type flap

Automatic
leading edge slat

Flap fully extended

Extended position

Trim tabs
riveted in place

Section A-A

Scale - mm   0   50   100   150   200   250

Scale - inches 0 1 2   4   6   8   10

CONTROL SURFACE MOVEMENTS

Stabilizer adjustment - 3°±30' up, 6°±30' down
Rudder - 30°±2° left, 30°±2° right
Elevator - 35°±2° up, 35°±2° down
Flaps - 55°+1° - 5° down
Ailerons - 20°±2° up, 20°±2° down

Aerial omitted for clarity

Canopy hinged
starboard side

Main landing gear
pivot point

Gun camera window

Whip
aerial

Grateful acknowledgement and appreciation are extended
to the following, who were able to assist and provide the
necessary information to make an exact scale drawing
of this aircraft possible.

Messerschmitt-Bölkow-Blohm GmbH, Ottobrunn, Germany
Deutsches Museum, Munich, Germany
Air Force Museum, Wright-Patterson A.F.B., Ohio
E.T. Maloney and "Planes of Fame" Museum, Chino, Calif.

MESSERSCHMITT ME-262A-1a
© By Kenneth S. Bokelman 1975

Sheet 1 of 2

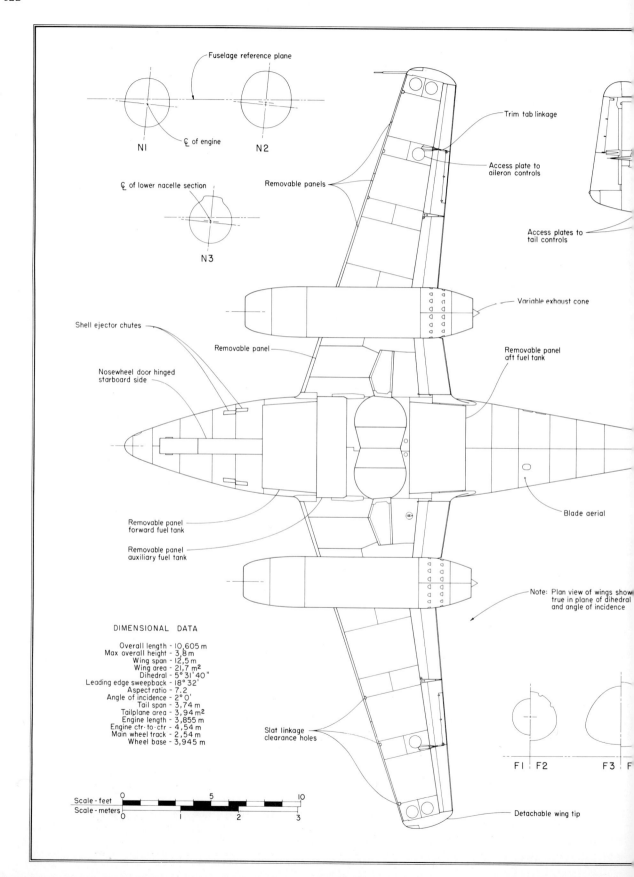

Fuselage reference plane

₵ of engine

N1   N2

₵ of lower nacelle section

N3

Removable panels

Trim tab linkage

Access plate to
aileron controls

Access plates to
tail controls

Variable exhaust cone

Shell ejector chutes

Removable panel

Removable panel
aft fuel tank

Nosewheel door hinged
starboard side

Blade aerial

Removable panel
forward fuel tank

Removable panel
auxiliary fuel tank

Note: Plan view of wings show
true in plane of dihedral
and angle of incidence

DIMENSIONAL DATA

Overall length - 10,605 m
Max overall height - 3,8 m
Wing span - 12,5 m
Wing area - 21,7 m²
Dihedral - 5° 31' 40"
Leading edge sweepback - 18° 32'
Aspect ratio - 7.2
Angle of incidence - 2° 0'
Tail span - 3,74 m
Tailplane area - 3,94 m²
Engine length - 3,855 m
Engine ctr·to·ctr - 4,54 m
Main wheel track - 2,54 m
Wheel base - 3,945 m

Slat linkage
clearance holes

F1 F2   F3 F

Scale - feet   0   5   10
Scale - meters   0   1   2   3

Detachable wing tip

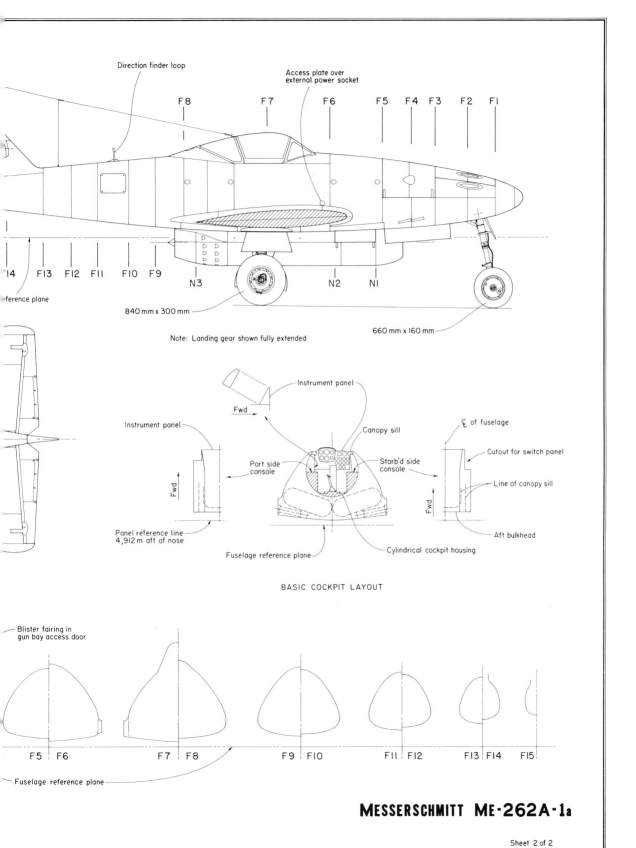

Direction finder loop

Access plate over
external power socket

F8   F7   F6   F5 F4 F3   F2   F1

F13 F12 F11 F10 F9   N3   N2   N1

ference plane

840 mm x 300 mm

660 mm x 160 mm

Note: Landing gear shown fully extended

Instrument panel

Fwd

Instrument panel

Canopy sill

₵ of fuselage

Fwd

Port side
console

Starb'd side
console

Cutout for switch panel

Line of canopy sill

Fwd

Panel reference line
4,912 m aft of nose

Fuselage reference plane

Cylindrical cockpit housing

Aft bulkhead

BASIC COCKPIT LAYOUT

Blister fairing in
gun bay access door

F5   F6   F7   F8   F9   F10   F11   F12   F13 F14   F15

Fuselage reference plane

MESSERSCHMITT ME-262A-1a

Sheet 2 of 2

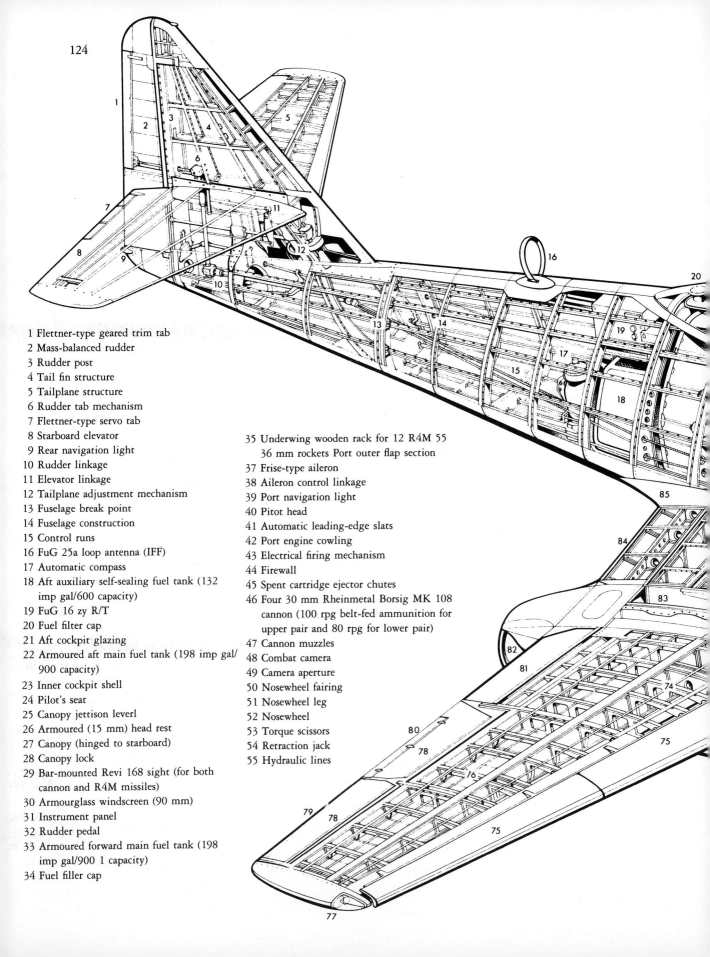

124

1 Flettner-type geared trim tab
2 Mass-balanced rudder
3 Rudder post
4 Tail fin structure
5 Tailplane structure
6 Rudder tab mechanism
7 Flettner-type servo tab
8 Starboard elevator
9 Rear navigation light
10 Rudder linkage
11 Elevator linkage
12 Tailplane adjustment mechanism
13 Fuselage break point
14 Fuselage construction
15 Control runs
16 FuG 25a loop antenna (IFF)
17 Automatic compass
18 Aft auxiliary self-sealing fuel tank (132
   imp gal/600 capacity)
19 FuG 16 zy R/T
20 Fuel filter cap
21 Aft cockpit glazing
22 Armoured aft main fuel tank (198 imp gal/
   900 capacity)
23 Inner cockpit shell
24 Pilot's seat
25 Canopy jettison leverl
26 Armoured (15 mm) head rest
27 Canopy (hinged to starboard)
28 Canopy lock
29 Bar-mounted Revi 168 sight (for both
   cannon and R4M missiles)
30 Armourglass windscreen (90 mm)
31 Instrument panel
32 Rudder pedal
33 Armoured forward main fuel tank (198
   imp gal/900 1 capacity)
34 Fuel filler cap

35 Underwing wooden rack for 12 R4M 55
   36 mm rockets Port outer flap section
37 Frise-type aileron
38 Aileron control linkage
39 Port navigation light
40 Pitot head
41 Automatic leading-edge slats
42 Port engine cowling
43 Electrical firing mechanism
44 Firewall
45 Spent cartridge ejector chutes
46 Four 30 mm Rheinmetal Borsig MK 108
   cannon (100 rpg belt-fed ammunition for
   upper pair and 80 rpg for lower pair)
47 Cannon muzzles
48 Combat camera
49 Camera aperture
50 Nosewheel fairing
51 Nosewheel leg
52 Nosewheel
53 Torque scissors
54 Retraction jack
55 Hydraulic lines

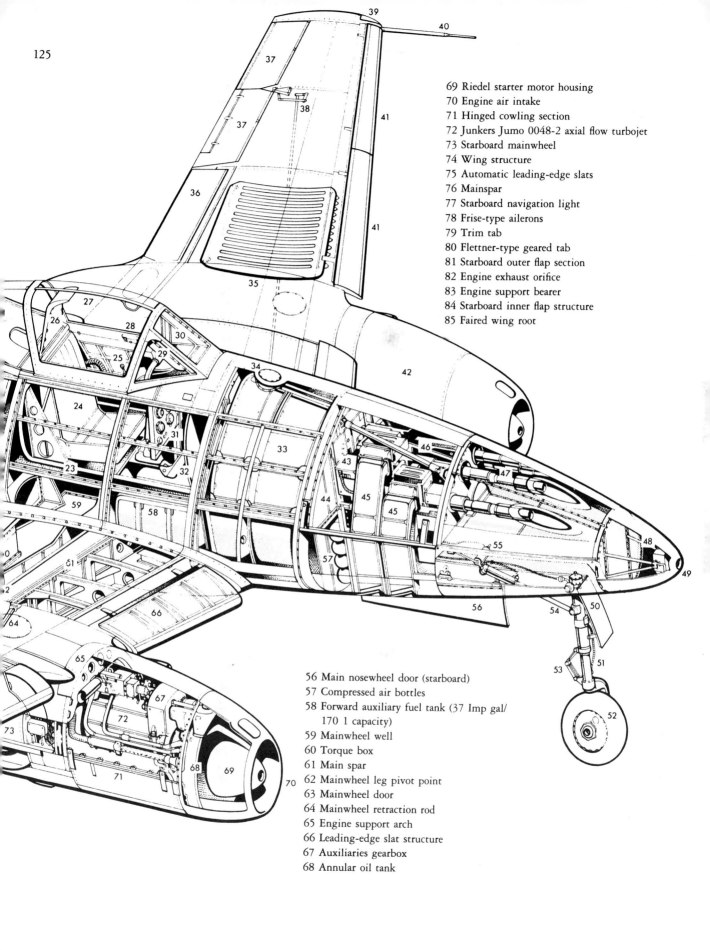

125

69 Riedel starter motor housing
70 Engine air intake
71 Hinged cowling section
72 Junkers Jumo 0048-2 axial flow turbojet
73 Starboard mainwheel
74 Wing structure
75 Automatic leading-edge slats
76 Mainspar
77 Starboard navigation light
78 Frise-type ailerons
79 Trim tab
80 Flettner-type geared tab
81 Starboard outer flap section
82 Engine exhaust orifice
83 Engine support bearer
84 Starboard inner flap structure
85 Faired wing root

56 Main nosewheel door (starboard)
57 Compressed air bottles
58 Forward auxiliary fuel tank (37 Imp gal/
   170 1 capacity)
59 Mainwheel well
60 Torque box
61 Main spar
62 Mainwheel leg pivot point
63 Mainwheel door
64 Mainwheel retraction rod
65 Engine support arch
66 Leading-edge slat structure
67 Auxiliaries gearbox
68 Annular oil tank

not be maintained in the best possible condition. The figures given are representative, rather than absolute, but they do give a good indication of the aircraft's amazing performance.

Color Codes

The exact color of an aircraft is always open for dispute, for there are significant variations in the actual color of paint prepared to the same specification, depending upon where and by whom it was manufactured, how it was mixed, over what it was applied, and how old it is. The following listing is believed to be the best representation of the actual colors of the Museum's aircraft:

AREA	COLOR	RLM CODE	MUNSELL CODE OR U.S. FEDERAL STANDARD 595A
Fuselage Primer	Gray		36559
Under Surface	Blue Gray	76	7.5B 7/2
Top Surface	Brown	81	10Y 3/2
Top Surface	Green	83	7.5GY 4/4
Landing Gear	Gray Green	02	10Y 5/2
Cockpit	Dark Gray	66	N3.0 (36076)
Plane Number	Yellow	04	2.5Y 8/12 (33538)
Bands	Yellow	27	5Y 7/10 (33481)
Band	Blue		5BP 2.5/6 (25053)
JG 7 Insignia	Red		7.5R 4/12
JG 7 Insignia	Blue		2.5 BP 4/8 (25102)

Fritz Wendel crawls into V056, a single place Me 262 A-1a experimentally fitted with the Lichtenstein S.N.2 radar and its Hirschgeweih antennae array. (Courtesy John Underwood)

OPPOSITE PAGE:

Colonel Watson in a 520mph fly past in a FE 110. A beautiful aircraft. (Major General Harold E. Watson)

*Only the declining war
situation prevented the
Germans from
manufacturing more of these
Me 262 B-1a/U1 night
fighters. Converted from the
Me 262 B-1a two seat
trainer, the aircraft had
two 66 Imperial gallon
auxiliary tanks attached
under the nose.*

Installation of the second seat required the rear main tank to be removed. The definitive night fighter, the Me 262 B-2a, had a longer fuselage so that the tank could be reinstalled.

<table>
</table>

| Equipment and Armament | The *Schwalbe* was fitted with a wide variety of equipment and armament, depending largely on the aircraft's function. Following is a brief listing intended to give a picture of the degree of flexibility and sophistication which characterized the Me 262. |

ITEM	DESCRIPTION
Cannons:	
MK 108	30 mm; standard weapon; 100 rounds per upper gun, 80 rounds per lower; poor trajectory; prone to jam
MK 103	30 mm; installed in ME 262 A-1a/U1
MG 151	20 mm; installed in Me 262 A-1a/U1 and Me 262 B-2a
MK 214A	55 mm; one installed in four experimental aircraft
Rockets:	
R4M	50 mm; weight 8.8 pounds; launched from simple wooden rack
X4	Wire guided; 132 pounds; not used operationally
Sights:	
Revi 16B	Standard *Luftwaffe* fighter gun sight
EZ 42	Gyroscopic sight produced by Askania;
Lotfe 7D	Standard *Luftwaffe* bombsight
GPV-1	Gegner-Pfeil-Visier (Flight Path Pointer) Sight for Air to Air bombing
TSA	Tief-und-Sturzflunganlage; for dive bombing
Bomb Racks:	
ETC 503	Standard *Luftwaffe* Unit
Wikingerschiff	Streamlined pylons
Bombs	*(Alternate Loads)*
1000 kg (2,200 lbs)	One only could be carried
500 kg (1,100 lbs)	Two could be carried
250 kg (550 lbs)	Two could be carried

Alternatively, either one 131.8 Imperial gallon or two 65.9 Imperial gallon drop tanks could be fitted.

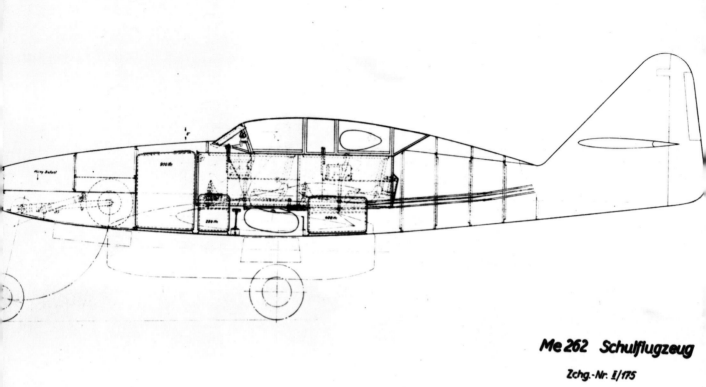

Me 262 Schulflugzeug

Zchg.-Nr. I/175

Messerschmitt A-G Augsburg   22.7.43

A somewhat rough drawing of the Me 262B-1a trainer's interior arrangement.

Radio and Radar:	(*Varied with aircraft type*)
SN-2 *Lichtenstein*	Used toasting fork antennae
FuG 218 *Neptun V*	Four pole radar array
FuG 240 *Berlin*	Dish scanner in nose reduced drag
FuG 16Z	Standard V.H.F. radio set
FuG 25a	Identification, Friend or Foe
FuG 120a	Automatic bearing indicator
FuG 125	Beam indicator for instrument approach (*Hermine*)
FuG 218	Airborne intercept equipment
FuG 350Zc *Naxos*	Homer for British H2S bombing equipment
Fug 120K	*Bernadine* directional indicator

Miscellaneous Gear:	
K-22 Auto pilot	Fitted to *Sturmvogels*
Cameras	Rb 50/30, Rb 20/30, Rb 75/30

CHAPTER 9

Contemporary Allied and Axis Jets

Allied Competitors

The Gloster E.28/39 was designed especially for the Whittle engine.

As with most wartime developments, the jet aircraft was not developed in isolation in Germany. In England, Sir Frank Whittle had anticipated Hans von Ohain's engine development, but had not been able to find a government or industry sponsor as ready to assist him in his revolutionary project as von Ohain had found with Heinkel. Whittle had first sought support in 1930, but it was not until 1935 that he was able to obtain limited commercial backing. Whittle and his backers formed Power Jets, Ltd., and struggled by on very limited amounts of money for the next four years to keep the company going and his test engines running. Government support was not given until May, 1938, and even then in a miserly fashion.

The prospect of war accelerated interest in Whittle's engine, which by 1939 was clearly a practical device, and with the increased support came increasing demands for rights in the engine, and for direction over its development. Notwithstanding some very difficult, and often unfair, negotiations, the government in July 1939 did promise Power Jets a contract for the full cost of construction of an engine designed for actual flight (later called the W-1) and simultaneously contracted with Gloster Aircraft Company for the design and construction of two airframes for flight test. Although intended only for experimental purposes, the E 28/39, as the new jet was designated, was supposed to be, as far as practical, based on the general needs for an interceptor.

The pressures of war had fanned British enthusiasm for the jet engine to the extent that Gloster was authorized early in 1940 to begin design work for a production jet fighter which would use the follow-on W-2 engine. This resulted in the famous Meteor, a twin jet fighter that served long and well for the R.A.F.

The E 28/39 first flew on May 15, 1941, the W-1 engine developing about 850 lbs of thrust. Speeds of 338 mph at 20,000 feet and 334 mph at 5,000 feet were attained. The success of Whittle's engine and the Gloster airframe convinced everyone in the Air Ministsry that the jet age was at hand, and the Meteor development received full support, despite a war situation which was anything but promising at the time.

The first flight of the Meteor took place from RAF Cranwell on March 5, 1943;

The Gloster Meteor was the first British jet to see combat, engaging V-1 Buzz bombs over England.

on July 21, 1944, just 16 months later, No. 616 squadron received its first two production aircraft, and on August 4, 1944, a Meteor flown by Flying Officer T. O. Dean scored its first confirmed victory by tipping a V-1 missile over with its wing tip.

On April 16, 1945, Meteor III aircraft from 616 Squadron undertook their first mission on the continent, flying from Nijmegen. Unfortunately for buffs and historians, no Meteors ever encountered a Messerschmitt Me 262 in combat, and the first jet versus jet battle would not occur until the Korean War.

The Meteor I was powered by two Rolls-Royce 1,700 lb static thrust Welland I engines, a development of the Power Jets W-2B. Slower than the Messerschmitt because of its greater frontal area, the Meteor was nonetheless a delightful aircraft to fly, and one that served the Royal Air Force well through the mid-1950s.

The inevitable question arises, of course, as to how the early Meteor and the *Schwalbe* might have fared in combat, given two pilots of equal caliber. The consensus is generally that the Me 262 would have been superior, on the basis of its greater speed and more lethal armament.

The American Jets

Despite the fact that America had spent years developing the successful turbo-supercharger, there was surprisingly little interest in the turbo-jet engine in the United States. Opie Chenoweth, a distinguished engineer at Wright Field, who pioneered in the development of 100 octane fuel, states that he often asked Dr. Stanford Moss, famous developer of the General Electric supercharger used so extensively in World War II, "Why he didn't see the connection between the supercharger and the jet engine—it was just a step away."

Nathan Price, at right, one of Americas most underrated engineers, was working on a promising jet engine just before W.W.II. Hal Hibbard, famed Lockeed designer, stands next to him.

According to Chenoweth, Moss's standard reply was, "Because I was dumb."

By 1939 two other inventors in the U.S. showed interest in the new engine, probably without knowledge of Whittle and von Ohain's work in Europe. A Czech immigrant, Vladimir H. Pavlecka developed a turboprop engine for Jack Northrop, called the Turbodyne, but a combination of things, including too high aspirations for the pressure ratios, lack of test facilities and limited company resources prevented successful development.

In 1940 an outstanding engineer about whose work too little has been written, Nathan C. Price, began work on the Lockheed L-1000, a true jet engine which was to be' developed in conjunction with an aircraft, the L-133. The combination was intended to fly at 625 mph at 50,000 feet and embodied many advanced concepts including reaction controls and boundary layer control. As in the case of the Turbodyne, however, the hoped-for efficiencies within the engine were beyond the state of the art, and the project was cancelled in 1941.

Jet aircraft development lagged in the United States until General Henry H. "Hap" Arnold made arrangements with the English for the manufacture of the Whittle engine in the United States. The Bell Aircraft Corporation of Buffalo was near enough to the General Electric plant to be selected to build the first fighter for the new engine.

A contract for three of the XP-59A fighters was awarded on September 5, 1941, less than four months after the first flight of the Gloster E 28/39 and ten months before the first flight of the Me 262.

The XP-59A Airacomet was a conventional looking aircraft, except for the absence of propellers, and with the absolute priority it had was completed in an amazingly short time. It took off from Muroc Dry Lake on October 2, 1942, headed into a completely undistinguished career.

This first American jet had a disappointing performance; with two 1,400 pound static thrust General Electric I-A engines, the aircraft had a maximum speed of 404 mph at 25,000, less than the best piston engine fighters of the time.

The program was continued, primarily to gain experience with jet aircraft, and 13 YP-59A and 100 P-59A aircraft were ordered. Half of the latter order was cancelled, and only 66 Airacomets were completed. The program was valuable to the U.S. Army Air Force, however, for it provided a great deal of knowledge which was applied in the later Lockheed XP-80, and a number of pilots were trained on the P-59.

The reason for the lack of performance is most apparent by looking at the Airacomet, which some pilots have likened to "a powered glider." There was too much frontal area, too much wing area, and a very "un-jet like" airfoil; in short, it was not a clean design.

The very advanced Lockheed L-133 jet fighter, which was to be designed and built with the Price engine.

The first American jet, the Bell XP-59A was not a successful fighter, but did provide a great deal of information on jet aircraft. The Germans mockingly called it the "Jet Storch".

XP-80

The first American operational jet fighter, the Lockheed XP-80, was a resounding success and led directly to a whole family of distinguished aircraft.

Lockheed took over development of a single engine jet fighter design from Bell, beginning work on the prototype on June 23, 1943. The aircraft flew 143 days later, on January 8, 1944, a remarkable achievement, and almost immediately demonstrated that it was everything that the XP-59A had not been. Shooting Star turned out to be a much more plausible nickname than Airacomet.

Designed by Kelly Johnson, the XP-80 had a top speed of 502 mph at 20,480 feet. It was powered by the first flight rated de Havilland H-1B Goblin engine, very generously sent by the R.A.F. to the United States at a time when its own jet program was in need of the engine.

Two XP-80As, equipped with the more powerful General Electric I-40 (later J33) engines of 3,850 lbs static thrust, were ordered, followed by 13 YP-80As for service test.

The plane was so promising that orders for 5,000 P-80As were placed; VJ day cut this back to 917.

Three of the YP-80As actually got to Europe, but did not see combat.

The XP-80 began a dynasty for Lockheed, for there were postwar orders for P-80Bs, P-80Cs, and the two seat trainer developments, the T-33 and TV-2. The aircraft lived on in the Lockheed F-94 *Starfire* series.

Postwar tests were conducted at Wright Field comparing performance of the Messerchmitt Me 262 and the Lockheed P-80A. The late Al Boyd ran the test, and the comparison was so favorable to the Me 262 that the results were suppressed.[1] The author found a copy only recently. The tests were not combat maneuvers, but comparisons of speed, rates of climb at different altitudes, and turning radius. The Messerschmitt had better speed and acceleration and an equal climb; the P 80 was easier to handle and had far better visibility.

(For further information on the Shooting Star, readers are referred to E.T. Wooldridge Jr's fine work *The Lockheed P-80*)

Germany

The emphasis placed on jet engine development in Germany resulted in a whole host of projects, ranging from the fast and maneuverable Heinkel He 280 fighter through the remarkably advanced Junkers Ju 287 six engine jet bomber. Only one aircraft type other than the Messerschmitt Me 262 actually reached operational status, however; this was the magnificent Arado Ar 234 bomber series. Other projects which reached varying stages of completion included the Heinkel He 162 *Volksjager*, a miniature jet fighter whose execution was far better than its conception; the ludicrous Messerschmitt Me 328, a pulse jet powered fighter which probably had more built-in vibration than any aircraft in history; the equally improbable Fieseler Fi 103 piloted V-1, the *Reichenberg,* a suicide weapon; the very advanced Messerschmitt P 1101, a testbed aircraft with a swing-wing capability, and the beautiful and promising Gotha Go 229 flying wing fighter.

Arado Ar 234. The Arado Ar 234A was an extremely clean shoulder wing monoplane of conventional construction, powered originally by two Junkers Jumo 004 engines, and capable of a top speed of 485 mph. The RLM had specified a long range for the aircraft, 1,340 miles, and the resulting fuel load requirement forced the designers to the unusual step of forgoing a conventional landing gear, and substituting instead a tricycle trolley for takeoff and retractable skids for landing.

The Ar 234 was hampered in development by the unavailability of flight tested engines, just as the Messerschmitt Me 262 was, and it did not make its first flight until June 15, 1943. The aircraft showed such promise, and the unorthodox landing arrangement was so inconvenient, that it was decided to redesign the fuselage to accommodate a conventional tricycle landing gear arrangement.

The Arado Ar 234 was as great a step forward in bombers as the Me 262 was in fighters. The aircraft was basically so sound that prototypes were pressed into operational missions. Top speed, clean, the speed was 457 mph at about 20,000 feet. With an externally mounted bomb, speed was reduced to 425 mph at the same altitude.

The revised aircraft, the Arado AR 234B *Blitz* was very advanced; the first prototype, flown on March 10, 1944, had both an ejection seat and a pressurized cockpit.

The *Luftwaffe's* need for fast reconnaissance was so great after the invasion, that experimental prototypes were pressed into operational use, with great success. The trickle of production Ar 234's provided the *Luftwaffe* with some additional bombing capacity as well. The aircraft could carry up to 3,300 pounds of bombs, and the pilot would set the aircraft on autopilot, switch hats, and become a bombardier, using the standard Lotfe 7K bomb sight. Defense armament was limited to two rear firing 20 mm cannon, aimed by the pilot through a periscope!

More than 200 Arado AR 234Bs were completed, and they proved to be a suitable companion to the Me 262. A final development, the Arado AR 234C series, was powered by four BMW 003 engines, and in one version had a top speed of 530 mph. The AR 234 was in every respect a formidable weapon, and it illustrates both the German genius for design and their almost inexplicable wartime penchant for frittering away a significant weapon in a series of interesting but wasteful experimental development efforts.

*Fieseler Fi 103
Reichenberg*

The Fieseler piloted V-1 bomb was a weapon conceived of equal measures of desperation and fanaticism. Its backers included the famed test pilot Hanna Reitsch, and the legendary S.S. leader, Otto Skorzeny, whose other feats included the rescue of Mussolini from the Gran Sasso, and the clandestine efforts associated with the Battle of the Bulge.

*The Fiesler Fi 103
"Reichenberg". This
desperation weapon was
essentially a piloted V-1
air launched from a mother
ship. Maximum speed was
a creditable 490 mph, but
the program was abandoned
after about 175 had been
built. (Peter B. Bowers
Collection)*

Basically a development of the V-1 missile, the *Reichenberg* had excellent one way performance, 490 mph for about 30 minutes, but it required the services of a carrier plane to get it within striking distance of Allied targets. By the time of its introduction in late 1944, it was almost impossible for *Luftwaffe* carrier planes to penetrate to within 250 miles of a profitable target. As a result the program was abandoned after about 175 of the diminutive aircraft had been produced, much to the relief of its prospective pilots.

*Gotha Go 229
(Horten Ho IX)*

Designed by two brothers, Walter and Reimar Horten, the jet powered flying wing *Horten* Ho IX was one of the most exotic looking aircraft of World War II.

The Hortens had experimented extensively with gliders and piston engine aircraft of the same all wing configuration, and the advent of the turbine engine opened new possibilities to them. They built two prototypes, designated *Horten* Ho IX V1 and Ho IX V2, and their performance was so promising that the *Gothaer Waggonfabrik* was assigned the task of developing the design for production.

The Horten Ho IX (V2), at Oranienburg in February, 1945, was a very successful all wing aircraft which achieved speeds of over 500 mph. It was reportedly delightful to fly. (Herbert Steinhower Collection)

The *Horten* Ho IX V2, powered by two Junkers Jumo 004B-1 engines, demonstrated a speed of more than 500 mph before its crash. The projected production aircraft, the *Gotha Go 229,* was a large aircraft for the day, with a wingspan of 54 feet 11 ¾ inches and a maximun loaded weight of 18,700 pounds. A maximum speed of 640 mph at 1,000 feet was predicted, with a service ceiling of 51,000 feet. A whole series of Go 229 prototypes were under construction, and had the war situation been stabilized, it is conceivable that they would have entered service in late 1945 or 1946.

The Museum is fortunate to have examples of both the Horten glider and the sole remaining *Horten* IX V3 (Go 229) prototype in its collection.

 143

The Gotha Go 229 was the production version of the Horten Ho IX V3. Never completed, it was expected to achieve a speed in excess of 600 mph and a ceiling of over 50,000 feet.

Heinkel He 280

The Heinkel He 280 was a very successful aircraft. With similar powerplants it was faster than the Me 262, but had less range and fire power. This is its first takeoff at Marienehe on April 1, 1941. The HeS 8A engine is uncowled' because of some fuel pooling problems.

The logical extension of Hans von Ohain's engine experiments, the Heinkel He 280 first flew on March 30, 1941. Powered by two HeS 8A jets of 1,290 pounds static thrust, the aircraft incorporated a number of innovations including a reliable tricycle landing gear and a pneumatic ejection seat.

Heinkel was enthralled with the aircraft, which ultimately had a top speed of over 500 mph, and was extremely maneuverable. The HeS 8 jet engines had significant problems, however, and the Messerschmitt Me 262 project overtook the He 280 development. By March of 1943 it was concluded that the Me 262, although marginally slower than the projected He 280, had a much greater range and a better armament package. Work on the He 280 was dropped, although various experimental efforts went on through the rest of 1944.

Heinkel He 162

The Heinkel He 162 *Volksjaeger* is an illustration of how competent engineers can retrieve the most embarrassing philosophical mistakes. The Heinkel He 162 requirement was conceived of by Nazi party functionaries as a parallel to the development of the *Volkstrum levee en masse* being perpetrated for the Army by Heinrich Himmler. The He 162 was to be a small aircraft, built largely of non-critical materials by unskilled workers, and flown by *Hitler Jugend* whose flight experience would be acquired as glider pilots! Forced by circumstances to make a serious response to the request for proposal, several German firms tendered designs. Heinkel, typically, proceeded with development of its design before any approval had been given, and as a result, the aircraft was designed and flown within 90 days.

The Heinkel He 162, here being test flown by a U.S.A.A.F. pilot, was a controversial fighter with excellent performance. Top speed with its single BMW 003 axial flow engine was 562 mph at about 20,000 feet altitude. The He 162 was tricky to fly, but in the hands of a competent pilot could have been a formidable adversary. (Peter M. Bowers)

Perhaps more surprising than the speed with which the *Volksjaeger* took the air was the manufacturing base created to produce it. Simultaneously with the design, a huge factory system had been set up with an ultimate capacity of 2,000 aircraft per month.

The airplane itself was highly unorthodox, with a tiny 23 ft 7½ in in span wing surmounting a cylindrical fuselage, and being in turn surmounted by a BMW 003 engine of 1,764 lbs static thrust. Top speed was 521 mph at about 20,000 feet; the aircraft was quite maneuverable, but it was far from easy to fly and it would have been murderous to place untrained pilots in it and expect them to enter combat. No Heinkel He 162's are known to have seen combat, although almost 300 reached flight status.

Henschel Hs 132A

Outwardly similar to the Heinkel He 162 in appearance, the Hs 132A was a ground attack aircraft which featured a prone pilot's position. The war ended before the aircraft could be flown.

At first glance similar to the Heinkel He 162, the Henschel Hs 132A was a prone position dive bomber intended to have a top speed of 485 mph. Like the Heinkel He 162 it was built largely of non-strategic material. The war ended before the aircraft flew. (Peter M. Bowers)

The Junker Ju 287 was to be a six engine jet bomber with forward swept wings. This, the Ju 287 V1, was a four engine prototype built in part with structures from other aircraft. The production aircraft was expected to have a top speed of 537mph at about 16,000 feet.

Junkers Ju 287

The most unusual characteristic of the four engined Junkers Ju 287 was its wings, which were swept forward at a 25 degree angle. Swept forward wings have some advantages over aft-swept wings in terms of low speed performance, and many advanced fighter projects have this feature.

A somewhat Frankensteinean version of this aircraft, the Ju 287V1, was flown on August 16, 1944. Using the fuselage of a Heinkel He 177, the tail of a Junkers Ju 388 and landing gear from a Junkers Ju 352 and a captured Consolidated B-24, the test bed proved the practicality of the swept forward wing, and encouraged the development of the Ju 287 V2, which was estimated to have had a performance of about 540 mph at medium altitudes. Once again the end of the war intervened, but in this case the components of the aircraft were transferred to Russia where it may have been flown.

Messerschmitt
Me 328

*The Messerschmitt Me
328, shown here mounted
on a Dornier Do 217E,
was powered by Argus As
014 pulse jets similar to
those used on V1 buzz
bombs. The aircraft was a
total failure.*

The Me 328 program was carried on for years with no visible signs of success.
Originally conceived of as a parasite fighter which would be towed behind heavy
bombers by the oft tried *Deichselschlepp* tow bar method, the Me 328 was successively
offered as a fighter, a fighter bomber, a suicide weapon similar to the *Reichenberg*
and finally, as an engineless fighter which would be towed to altitude to be released
for gliding attacks.

The entire project was predicated on the usefulness of Argus As 014 pulse jets
as an aircraft powerplant. They simply were not suitable, due to their inherent
vibration, and the project was abandoned, one more example of advocacy gone mad.

Messerschmitt P 1101

Dr. Woldemar Voigt, who had headed the Me 262 development effort, instituted design of the Messerschmitt *Project 1011* in July, 1942. The aircraft featured wings with a 40 degree sweepback, and a single jet engine mounted in a tadpole shaped body.

Wartime pressures prevented completion of the aircraft, which had gone through a curious cycle, from test aircraft to fighter prototype to test aircraft again. In early 1945 Voigt determined that the aircraft should be capable of three different ground adjustable sweep positions, thus anticipating the variable sweep aircraft of 20 years later. The changes in position were purely for experimental purposes, however. When the war ended, the aircraft was brought back to the United States. Robert Woods, the famous designer from Bell Aircraft pursued the design concept, and eventually a slightly larger version of the aircraft, the Bell X - 5, was flight tested in the U.S.

Italy

The Italian Caproni Campini received far more attention from a naive public than it deserved. Its propellerless flights attracted the press, despite the fact that its top speed was a modest 233 mph— hardly the vision of the jet age.

And it was not a jet in the ordinary sense of the word. A 900 horsepower Isotta Fraschini radial engine was mounted within the fuselage, driving a variable pitch, ducted fan compressor. Fuel was injected into the exhaust of the compressor, and this provided the thrust. The Campini was not a bad looking aircraft, but rather heavy and seemingly overstrength for its task. It has a 52 foot wing span, was 43 feet long, and had a maximum gross weight of 9,250 pounds. It made its first flight on August 28, 1940.

The Italian Caproni Campini was powered by a 900 horsepower Isotta Fraschim radial engine which drove a variable pitch ducted fan compressor. Top speed was 233 mph.

Several advanced versions of the aircraft were projected, but none came to fruition. The original aircraft is still in existence in the Caproni Museum.

150

Japan

The Japanese military attachés in Germany had witnessed test flights of the Messerschmitt Me 262 and had immediately notified the Naval Staff of the aircraft's potential. As a result, the Nakajima firm was assigned the task to create a plane, based on the *Schwalbe,* but with a much more modest performance. The performance requirements did not exceed the capability of contemporary piston engine fighters, for a speed of 432 mph, a range of 127 miles and a 551 pound bomb load was all that was called for.

The requirements were realistic in view of the very primitive state of jet engine development in Japan. As it developed, the engines for the Nakajima Kikka (Orange Blossom) were copies from the cross section diagram of a German engine.

The Japanese engine, the NE 20, developed 1,047 lbs of static thrust, adequate to achieve the desired performance.

The aircraft made its first flight on August 7, 1945, and was damaged a few days later on its second take-off. The end of the war in the Pacific closed the development process although one other aircraft was almost ready for flight, and there were several experimental and preproduction aircraft nearing completion. The only remaining Kikka now hangs in the same building at Silver Hill which houses the Boeing B-29 "Enola Gay," an interesting juxtaposition of types.

The Nakajima Kikka (Orange Blossom) was similar in planform to the Me 262, but was a much smaller aircraft. Design top speed was 432 mph. (Photo: Hideya Ando)

Me 262 Aircraft and Subtypes

AIRCRAFT/AIRCRAFT TYPE	COMMENTS
Me 262 V1 (PC + UA)	1st flight April 18, 1941, with piston engine.
Me 262 V2 (PC + UB)	Flown Oct. 2, 1942 on jet power.
Me 262 V3 (PC + UC)	First pure jet flight July 18, 1942; later crashed, repaired.
Me 262 V4 (PC + UD)	Flown by Galland; Junkers Jumo 004 A.
Me 262 V5 (PC + UE)	Fitted with fixed nose gear, Borsig rockets.
Me 262 V6 (VI + AA)	Powered by 004B engines; fully retractable tricycle gear.
Me 262 V7 (VI + AB)	Pressure cockpit.
Me 262 V8 (VI + AC)	Fitted with armament.
Me 262 V9 (VI + AD)	Communications equipment test. vehicle; some say was "High speed" version.
Me 262 V10 (VI + AE)	Experiments to reduce control forces; "towed" bombs.
Me 262 S1 (VI + AF)	Aerodynamic tests.
Me 262 S2 (VI + AG)	Usually assumed to be aircraft used for high speed tests.
Me 262A-1a	Fighter, *Schwalbe*, Jumo 004B1 B2 or B3 engines.
Me 262 A-1a/UI	Cannon armament test 2 20 mmMG 157, 2 30 mm MK 103, 2 30 mm MK 108.
Me 262A-1a/UI	1 50 mm Mauser MK 214 A.
Me 262A-1a/U2	Used *Hermine* Fug 125 bad weather instrument.
Me 262A-1a/U3	Reconnaissance nose; no armament.
Me 262A-1b	Carried 24 R4M rockets.
Me 262A-2a	*Sturmvogel* fighter-bomber; bomb pylons fitted.
Me 262A-2a/UI	Bomb dropping equipment (RSA) fitted.
Me 262A-2a/U2	Lotfe-7D Bomb Sight; wooden nose extension, two seater.
Me 262A-3a	Ground attack version; additional armor.
Me 262A-5a	Aux. fuel tanks, two camera Recce version; two cannon.
Me 262B-1a	Dual control two seat trainer; 15 built.
Me 262B-1a/UI	Trainers converted to night fighters.

The Royal Air Force's Me 262 A-1a at Hendon, outside London. Aircraft is now indoors (Courtesy Jack Bruce RAF Museum). This photograph, and all the following ones, are of surviving Me 262's.

Me 262B-2a	Radar equipped, Schrage Musik, night fighter; lengthened fuselage, aux. tanks.
Me 262C-1a	*Heimatschutzer* I rocket boosted fight.
Me 262C-2b	*Heimatschutzer* II BMW 003 and rocket boost.
Me 262C-3	Jettisonable rocket engine and tanks.
S-92	Czechoslovakian Me 262A-1b.
CS-92	Czechoslovakian Me 262B-1a.

SURVIVORS	COMMENTS
Me 262 A-1b	National Air and Space Museum, Washington, D.C. Restored.
Me 262A-1a	Air Force Museum, Dayton, Ohio. Restored.
Me 262 A-1a	Royal Air Force Museum, Hendon, England, Work Number 112372, Restored.
Me 262 A-1a/U3	Maloney's Planes of Fame, Chino, California, Awaiting Restoration.
Me 262 A-1a	Deutsches Museum, Munich Germany, Work Number 500071, Restored.
Me 262 B-1a	Willow Grove NAS, needs work, Work Number 110639.
Me 262 A-2a	Australian War Memorial, Canberra, Work Number 500210.
Me 262 B-1a/UI	South African National Museum, Saxonwold, Transvaal.
Avia S92	National Technical Museum, Prague.
Me 262 B-1a	National Technical Museum, Prague

The Air Force Museum aircraft has been recently restored. (Air Force photo)

The Australian Me 262 A-1a stands next to its even rarer World War I compatriot, the Albatros D.Va. (Courtesy Australian War Memorial)

154

The Deutches Museums Me 262 A-1a spent years in Switzerland before being returned. (Courtesy Deutches Museum)

The two seat Me 262 B-1a/U. of the South African Natural Museum is beautifully restored. (Courtesy S.A. National Museum of Military History)

The Me 262 B-1a at NAS Willow Grove has been in outside storage for years. Formerly designated 121448 by U.S. Navy. Aircraft is claimed by some to be a Me 262 B-1a/U., FE 610.

155

The Messerschmitt Me 262 B-1a formerly seen at Brno, Czechoslavakia, in 1966. Reportedly now restored and inside the technical museum.

The postwar Czechoslovakian Avia S.92 version of the Me 262. (Courtesy Narodni Technicke Muzeum, Prague)

Ed Maloney's Me 262, the former FE 4012 at Planes of Fame Museum, Chino, California. (Courtesy Ed Maloney)

Roll out day for the National Air and Space Museum Me 262.

Me 262 Chronology

DATE	EVENT
February 1936	Dr. Hans von Ohain hired by Ernst Heinkel.
1937	Von Ohain demonstration engines run.
April 1938	RLM gives contract to Messerschmitt for jet airframes.
December 1938	Mauch and Schelp set up formal reaction powerplant program; Antz sets up similar airframe program.
June 7, 1939	Messerschmitt submits technical proposal on Me 262, "project 1065"; Rudolph Seitz undertakes 262 design.
August 27, 1939	First flight of Heinkel He 178, Erich Warsitz, pilot.
December 19, 1939	*Projekt* 1065 mockup inspection.
March 1, 1940	Contract let for three flight test and one static test airframe of Me 262.
May 15, 1940	Changes in engine size forces redesign of Me 262; engines to be placed under wing.
July 1940	Junkers begins Junkers Jumo 004 engine development.
August 1940	Construction begins on Me 262 prototypes.
August 1940	BMW engine, 003 prototype runs.
November 1940	Junkers Jumo 004A test engine runs, major problems encountered.
January 1941	Me 262 prototypes completed; no engines available.
March 30, 1941	Heinkel He 280 jet fighter flies.
April 18, 1941	First prototype Me 262 262 VI (PC + UA) flies on piston engine power; several flights made subsequently.
May 15, 1941	Gloster E 28/39 first flight.
Summer 1941	BMW 003 engine flight tested.
July 25, 1941	Contract for five test and 20 preproduction Me 262's.
November 25, 1941	Me 262 VI flies with piston and jet engines; jet engines fail.

March 15, 1942	Junkers Jumo 004A flight tested under Bf 110.
July 18, 1942	First flight Me 262/V3 (PC + UC) on jet power only.
August 17, 1942	Me 262/V3 crashed.
October 1942	Me 262 V2 (PC + UB) joins test program.
October 2, 1942	Bell XP-59A first flight.
December 2, 1942	Me 262 production targeted at 20 per month.
February 11, 1943	Me 262 test fuselage drop tested from Me 323.
March 2, 1943	Me 262 VI flies under pure jet power.
March 5, 1943	First flight Gloster Meteor.
May 22, 1943	Galland flies Me 262; gives glowing endorsement.
June 2, 1943	Me 262 released for mass production.
June 26, 1943	First flight of Me 262 V5, equipped with fixed nose wheel.
August 17, 1943	Me 262 jigs destroyed in bombing raid on Regensburg.
October 1943	Junkers Jumo 004B-1 engines flight tested on Me 262.
November 1943	Goering inquires if Me 262 can be used as bomber.
November 26, 1943	Me 262 V3 with fully retractable tricycle gear demonstrated to Adolph Hitler.
December 1943	Me 262 V6 (UI + AB) tests pressure cockpit.
December 12, 1943	Hitler calls for commitment of Me 262 as fighter bomber.
December 1943	Albert Speer gives Me 262 top production priority.
December 1943	Erpobungskommando 262 starts training.
January 8, 1944	First flight Lockheed XP-80.
March 1944	Jagerstab (Fighter Staff) set up to accelerate Me 262 production.
April 1944	First 16 pre-production Me 262's accepted by Luftwaffe.
April 1944	First operational sorties by Me 262.
May 1944	Program 223 deliveries schedules for 60 Me 262's monthly.
May 1944	Me 262 V10 tests bomb pylons.
June 8, 1944	Notorious Fuhrerbehfel limits Me 262 production to bomber version.
July 6, 1944	Me 262 S2 VI + AG reportedly flies at 624 mph.
July 1944	Sturmvogel fighter bomber deliveriesbegin.
July 25, 1944	Mosquito reports encounter with Me 262.
August 28, 1944	1st USAAF victory over Me 262.
August 30, 1944	Hitler allows every 20th Me 262 to be built as fighter.
August 1944	Kommando Schenck does operational sorties over France.
October 3, 1944	Kommando Nowotny achieves operational status.

October 1944	KG 51 operational, makes bombing attacks on Nijmegen bridge.
November 2, 1944	Me 262 uses R4M rockets in combat.
November 4, 1944	Me 262 now to be built as fighter.
November 8, 1944	*Major* Nowotny shot down.
December 1944	Me 262 air to air bomb tests conducted at Rechlin.
December 1944	Reconnaissance unit *Sonderkommando Braunegg* formed.
December 1944	*Kommando Welter* formed; renamed 10/NJG 11 in February; later use Me 262-1a/U1 night fighters.
January 1945	*Jagdverband* 44 formed under *Generalleutnant* Adolf Galland.
February 25, 1945	KG(J)54 loses seven Me 262s in combat.
February 27, 1945	Me 262c-1a *Heimatschutzer* I (Home Defense I) rocket boosted aircraft tested.
March 1, 1945	Heavy jet attack; 25 Me 262s strike 8th AF over Dresden.
March 18, 1945	Thirty-seven Me 262s attack over Berlin.
March 31, 1945	Jv 44 operational at base at Munchen Riem.
April 10, 1945	25 to 30 Me 262s destroyed in worst day of war for *Schwalbe* squadrons.
April 26, 1945	Galland's last sortie.
May 3, 1945	JV 44 ceases operations.

Luftwaffe Units Known to Have Used the Me 262

UNIT	COMMENTS
Eprobungskommando 262	Test unit, at Lechfeld 2 Staffeln.
Kommando Nowotny	Commanded by *Major* Nowotny. Operated 3 Oct. to 8 Nov. 1944
Kommando Schenk	Conversion unit for bomber pilots, ex KG 51.
I./KG 51	First *Gruppe* KG 51 operationalin Oct. 1944, *Luftflotte* 3.
KG 51 (*Geschwader Stab*)	Staff unit of KG 51.
II./KG 51	Second *Gruppe* KG 51. Also under *Luftflotte* 3.
Kommando Edelweis	Experimental unit using KG 51 pilots.
Jagdgeschwader 7	All three *Gruppen* became operational to some degree along with the *Geschwaderstabb*.
Jagdgruppe 10	Developed R4M Rockets.
III./*Erganzungs-jagdgeschwader/JG2*	*Sturmvogel* training unit at Lechfeld.
KG(J)6	Entered 262 training; Parts of III *Gruppe* became operational.
KG(J)27	Entered 262 training; not operational.
KG(J)30	Entered 262 training; not operational.
IV./*Erganzungsjagdgeschwader/KG51*	Replacement Training unit for KG 51.
Kommando Stamp	Experimental Night Fighter Unit defending Berlin.
Kommando Welter	*Kommando Stamp* redesignated.
NJG/11	*Kommando Welter* redesignated.
I./KG(J)54	Converted Ju 88 unit. Became operational.
Einsatz Kommando Braunegg	Reconnaissance unit.
Nahaufklarungsgruppe 6	Formed from *Kommando Braunegg*.
1/Versuchsverband Ob. d.l.	Special experimental unit.
Jagdverband 44	Galland's elite unit.
I./*Erganzungsjagdgeschwader/KG(J)*	Training unit.
II./*Erganzungsjagdgeschwader/KG(J)*	Training unit.

APPENDIX **D**

𝕱𝖗𝖎𝖙𝖟 𝖂𝖊𝖓𝖉𝖊𝖑'𝖘 𝖋𝖑𝖎𝖌𝖍𝖙 𝕹𝖔𝖙𝖊𝖘

(DIRECT TRANSLATION)

While the standard Luftwaffe and USAF pilot's notes on handling the Me 262 have been previously available, this is the first time that the recommendations of Messerschmitt's most famous test pilot have been published.

Wendel made the first flight in the Me 262 and was subsequently a major figure in the test program. Other Messerschmitt and Luftwaffe test pilots who should be mentioned include Karl Baur, Willy Hoffman, Dipl. Ing. Heinrich Beauvis, Wolfgang Spate, Herr Ostertag, and Gerd Linder.

A.1.2.(g) Report No. 2357

HANDLING THE ME 262

Several Me 262 aircraft have been captured intact and will be flown by Allied test pilots. In view of this some notes which have been obtained from the Offices of Messerschmitt at Augsburg have been translated by this section and are reproduced below:

PILOTS NOTES ON ME 262 BY FLUG KAPITAN WENDEL

In addition to studying the condensed instructions for airframe and engines, a thorough knowledge of these notes, preferably before the first flight in an Me 262, is essential to the pilot.

1. *Taxiing*

Always accelerate the engines slowly. The gas temperature must never rise above the permitted value and the engine must not "roar" *(bullern)*. In view of this, only take corners by using the brakes, never by using the engines. Always taxi gently and never make sharp turns, otherwise control of the aircraft will be lost.

2. *Take-off*

Switch on the fuel pumps in the main tanks. Hold the aircraft stationary by applying the brakes and then slowly run up the engines, especially slowly up to 7,500 r.p.m. The brakes must be so adjusted that they will hold the aircraft stationary up to 8,500 r.p.m.

    After releasing the brakes, push the throttle lever right forward and then check over the engine. The aircraft makes so little demand upon the pilot at the commencement of the take-off run that he is easily able to carry out this check. The check is done by eye and ear, the engines must not "roar" and the instruments must show the same values as they did during running up or during previous take-offs. The gas pressure must be especially watched, and if it is more than five per cent lower than previously, do not take-off. In such a case, it is most likely that cavitation has taken place in one of the compressor stages, that is, by running up too quickly, the compressor has been overloaded and the smooth flow breaks up, exactly as it does when a wing stalls. Cavitation takes place so easily in many compressors as a result of small constructional faults or as a result of foreign bodies that they become entirely unserviceable. If the take-off is continued when cavitation has occurred in the compressor, then the quantity of air flowing through is too small, the quantity of fuel injected however is the same or sometimes even larger, as a result of which, the engine is overheated.

The directional corrections during take-off should only be made with the brakes.

The control column should remain in the neutral position.

The angle of attack of the wing, when running on all three wheels, is smaller than the angle of attack when flying at the lowest possible speed (after becoming airborne). As a result of this, when the aircraft has reached the lowest permissible flying speed, the angle of attack must be increased, in other words, the aircraft must be pulled away from the ground. If the stick is pulled back too soon, or if, at the right speed, it is pulled back too far, then there is only a rise in resistance, but no increase in lift, in fact, there may be a lessening of lift. The aircraft cannot then climb. In this case immediately reduce the angle of attack to the "running" angle, in other words, push the stick forward and then start the process again.

When will the aircraft be pulled off the ground? It is best to go by the A.S.I. which should read with a fighter, fully laden i.e. 6,700 kg., 190 - 200 k.p.h. with a bomber, fully laden i.e. 7,100 kg., 200 - 220 k.p.h. After becoming airborne, immediately push the stick forward slightly as the required elevator angle for pulling off the ground is greater than that for climbing at the slowest speed.

Essential for a perfect take-off is correct setting of the tailplane. *The tailplane must always be trimmed nose heavy!* The further back the centre of gravity moves, the more nose heavy it must be trimmed. When the 600 litre fuel tank is full, the center of gravity is at its rearmost position. The tailplane must then be set at $+2 X - +3°$ (i.e. 4 - 6 graduations on the indicator).

3. Rocket Take-Off

In order to shorten the take-off run, the rockets should be ignited 40 - 30 k.p.h. before the optimum take-off speed. If the take-off run need not be shorter, but there are obstacles to be negotiated after becoming airborne, then only ignite the rockets later, possibly even leaving it until the aircraft is airborne. Jettison the take-off rockets at low speeds, otherwise damage may be caused to the fuselage.

4. Operation of undercarriage and landing flaps

The undercarriage and landing flaps are hydraulically operated. The hydraulic pump has a capacity of 18 litres/min. and is attached to the port engine. Its capacity is rather too low and it is intended to fit an 18 litre per minute pump on the starboard engine. In the present state, therefore, the undercarriage operates very slowly. This is particularly noticeable when lowering. The nose wheel comes down very much later than the main undercarriage; so lower in plenty of time. The high speed of the aircraft easily tempts one to lower the undercarriage of flaps whilst travelling too fast and this leads to damage. The *permissible operating speed must be rigidly adhered to.*

5. *Emergency operation*

Compressed air is used for emergency operation of the undercarriage and it lowers the nose wheel and the main undercarriage fairing. The undercarriage itself falls under the influence of gravity. If it does not immediately lock, then assist it by side slipping.

6. *Warning*

The compressed air is only admitted to the undercarriage or flaps after two full turns of the operating handle have been made. With emergency operation both undercarriage and flaps lower more quickly.

7. *Flight*

Always climb at the optimum climbing speed, never more slowly. The best speeds are given in the table below.

        0 m. altitude speed 475 k.p.h. (true)
    2,000 m.   ”   ”   500   ”   ”
    4,000 m.   ”   ”   525   ”   ”
    6,000 m.   ”   ”   550   ”   ”
    8,000 m.   ”   ”   600   ”   ”
    10,000 m.   ”   ”   650   ”   ”

Note: The Me 262 has an altitude compensated A.S.I. and, therefore, the indicated speed is equivalent to the true speed above 400 k.p.h.

The highest permissible rearward point for the centre of gravity is 30 percent of the mean aerodynamic wing chord. If this position is exceeded, then the aircraft becomes unstable about the lateral axis, that is, it does not remain trimmed, but will automatically stall in a turn. Under normal conditions of fuel stowage this position is not exceeded, but it is necessary always to watch most carefully the transfer pumping instructions. Watch particularly that the main tanks do not overflow as the J-2 fuel will run out into the fuselage and get on the wireless equipment which interferes with radio traffic.

When cruising, the tailplane must be between 0 and +2°.

8. *Directional Stabililty*

When the center of gravity is far back and the Flettner rudder trimming tabs are not perfect, especially if the Flettner tabs are a little too thick, then the aircraft sways about the vertical axis. This movement must stop when both legs are pushed hard against the rudder pedals. If this does not stop the movement then the tabs must be altered or the trailing edge of the rudder must be bent slightly outwards. A modification is in course of preparation.

9. *Landing*

The best approach speed is 230 - 250 k.p.h. Shortly before reaching the airfield boundary, decrease the glide angle a little and reduce the speed to about 200 k.p.h. Then flatten out and touch down normally as with an aircraft having a tail wheel. Touch-down speed is 175 k.p.h. After touch-down, allow the aircraft to tip forward slowly. Only apply brakes when the nose wheel has touched the ground.

10. *Going round again*

It is just as easy to go round again as with other types of aircraft, but is must be remembered that by approaching slowly the engine revolutions are low, and just as at take-off, the throttle lever must only be moved forward slowly.

11. *Single Engine Flight*

When flying on one engine only, a turning moment is developed about the vertical axis, due to the engine being offset from the longitudinal axis of the aircraft. The amount of this moment is dependent upon the power and the leverage. In this case the leverage remains constant, but the power (i.e. the effect of the running engine) changes. In order that the aircraft may remain on course, this moment must be offset, which is done by applying rudder. The amount of rudder applied must be sufficient to keep the ball of the turn and bank indicator in the center; note this particularly in turns. Turns can be made either with or against the stationary engine. During long single-engine flights the force on the rudder pedal may be reduced by adjusting the Flettner trimming tabs.

The turning moment imparted by the specific movement of the rudder is dependent on air-flow pressure. The smaller the pressure, the greater must be the rudder movement. In single-engine flight, with retracted undercarriage, the speed is something over 500 k.p.h. at full throttle. In this case only about ⅓ of the possible rudder movement is necessary. This low speed, however, can only occur at full throttle if one is climbing at too great an angle or if the undercarriage has been lowered.

12. *Single Engine landings*

From what has previously been said, it will be seen that the following is necessary for a single-engine landing; minimum approach speed 260 k.p.h., so that, if necessary, full throttle may be given. At this speed and with one engine at full throttle, the aircraft loses height with lowered undercarriage, but raised flaps at 1 - 2 ms/sec. From this, it will be seen that the undercarriage should only be lowered at such a time that it is possible to reach the airfield with little or no aid from the engine. Approach speed 260 k.p.h. About 500 ms. before reaching the airfield (when too high earlier, when too low later) lower the flaps and complete the landing in a normal manner. Side slipping is possible. When landing, the Flettner trimming tabs should be set in the neutral position. If it is necessary to approach under power, then the necessary force on the rudder must be exerted by the pilot. At full throttle under all circumstances apply full rudder.

A.I.2.(g)
D. of I. (R)
25th May, 1945

H. G. MORISON
Squadron Leader for Wing Commander.

A Contemporary Internal Messerschmitt History

by RAKAN KOKOTHAKI

(DIRECT TRANSLATION)

This story of the Messerschmitt A. G., written by the vice president of the firm at the war's end, is valuable for the perspective it provides of the company's existence and method of operation.

Rakan Kokothaki's business ability was a perfect complement to Willy Messerschmitt's engineering skills. It was Kokothaki who obtained valuable contracts at times when the firm desperately needed them, and who made financially possible Messerschmitt's sometimes extravagant engineering challenges, and who perceived first and most strongly the critical importance of the Me 262 to Germany.

Written at a time when simultaneously his firm had witnessed its greatest technological achievements and his nation its greatest defeat, the account adds important insight to the Messerschmitt story. It reveals the almost continuous financial infighting that beset Messerschmitt from the beginning, and chronicles his eventual - if short lived - triumph. The account is a little hard to read, but it is source material from a principal participant given at the time.

A commentary on Messerschmitt's financial operations is given by famed U.S., Aircraft Manufacturer Lawrence D. Bell following Mr. Kokothaki's review.

The original name of the Messerschmitt A. G. was Bayerische Flugzeugwerke A. G. (BFW). The main office was in Augsburg. The BFW A. G. was founded in Munich on July 30, 1926.

The founders were -
> The German Reich
> The Bavarian State

and the banking house Merek, Finsk & Co. The stock of the company was worth RM 400,000.

It was divided as follows:

The founders were - German Reich - represented by the Reich's
Transportation Minister -
RM 250,000

Bavarian State - represented by the
Bavarian Trade Ministry -
RM 100,000

Banking House Merek, Finsk & Co. Munich -
RM 50,000

The principal reason in the founding of the BFW - A.G. was the fact that it was intended to take over both the assets and liabilities of the Udet - Flugzeugbau G. m. b. H. in Munich - Ramersdorf.

The Udet - Flugzeugbau G. m. b. H. in Munich had since 1923 been engaged in the development and the construction of the training and transport planes. Herein the banking house of Merek, Finsk & Co. had made several large loans. It was not possible for the company to achieve an economic basis, so that it finally had to rely on the banking house Merek, Finsk & Co., as well as the Bavarian State and the Reich's Transportation Ministry in Berlin for support. The banking house of Merek, Finsk & Co. had alone invested RM $800,000 towards the end of July, 1926. It was impossible to get any dividends from the total enterprise.

The negotiations with the Reich's Travel Ministry and the Bavarian State led to the result that a new company was founded, namely the Bayerische Flugzeugwerke A. G. which had to take over the economic ruin of the Udet - Flugzeugbau G. m. b. H.

Along with the founding of a new company, a change in the location of the main office was also planned. In the spring of 1926 the Udet - Flugzeugbau attempted to negotiate with the Eisenwek Gebruder Frisch in order to acquire the property of the former Rumplerwerke A. G. in Augsburg. It was in July, 1926, that the contract was drawn up but was not signed. The Udet - Flugzeugban was not in a position financially to go through with the deal.

The newly founded company of BFW - A. G. therefore went through with this contract and dealt anew with the Eisenwerk Gebruder Frisch, after which it moved with the collective equipment of the Udet - Flugzeugbau G. m. b. H. to Augsburg. Naturally with the founding of the new company, radical changes were brought about in the management. The chief construction and development engineer from the Udet - Flugzeugbau G. m. b. H., a Mr. Hermann, was kept. But the manager of the Udet - Flugzeugbau G. m. b. H., a Mr. Pohl, was not retained because it was believed his was the principal fault for the economic instability of the enterprise. Pohl had previously already squeezed out his two partners Ernest Udet and Scheuermann.

The move to Augsburg began on the 2nd of August 1926 (the author started in with the BFW on the 13th of August, 1936). The management of the BFW - A.G. was entrusted to Dr. Alexander Schruffer. The first meeting of the stockholders was as follows:

General Direktor, Franz Josef Popp, Bayerische Motorenwerke A. G. Munich

Ministerialrat, Muhlig Hofnan, Reichsverkehraministerium Berlin

Ministerialrst, Dr. Hellman Bayr, Staataministerfum fur Handel & Industrie Munich

Reshsanwalt, Hoffman von Bankhaus Merek, Finsk & Co. Munich

Ministerialrat, Dr. Panzeran von Reischafinanaministerium, Berlin

Oberregierungerat, Blum Reichafinans, Munich

While the company was being founded, the debts, which had been insured by the Udet - Flugzeugbau G. m. b. H. to an amount of RM 23,000, were paid off to the Banking House of Merek, Finsk & Co. Tied together with this balancing of accounts, the Reich's Travel Ministry lent the BFW - A.G. a sum of RM 400,000 in addition to the original investment. This loan was payable on immediate call at an interest of 5% yearly.

The BFW - A.G. had many expenses because of the acquisition of the land and buildings of the former Rumplerwerke Augsburg, and the improvements and repairs on them, and also the moving of the Udet - Flugzeugbau G. m. b. H. from Munich - Ramersdorf to Augsburg.

Besides this, manufacturing could only be started toward the end of 1926. Through this further losses were insured, otherwise the newly formed company had been outfitted with a total loan of RM 423,000, which was not for all uses, but for the covering of the debt to Merek, Finsk & Co. Therefore, the economic result was actually a total loss.

On the 10th of January, 1927, the new specialist of the company, Prokurist Fritz Hille (formerly Director of the Bayerische Motorenwerke A. G. Munich) had clearly presented the situation to the meeting of the shareholders and thereby achieved the point that the Reich's Travel Ministry changed its loan to an outright gift. This subsidy was even increased by RM 90,000 from the Reich's Travel Ministry and by RM 25,000 from Merek, Finsk and Co. to a grand total of RM 515,000. This subsidy was given on the condition that the banking house of Merek, Finsk & Co. was to be ousted from the partnership. Its shares of RM 50,000 were to be added to those of the Reich's Travel Ministry.

The BFW planned a manufacturing program first off, of a mass-production of a training plane "Flamingo" V12 A & B, developed by the Udet - Flugzeugbau. The contracts were distributed by the Reich's Travel Ministry. The wood-constructed training plane was to be further developed in mixed construction, if possible, keeping the original form. It was therefore intended that the fuselage be made by welded steel construction, while the wings remained wood constructed. The Chief Engineer Hermann had many differences of opinion with this firm which finally led to his dismissal in the Fall of 1926. Therefore, the development department remained without a leader and without an important personality for technical development.

During the same time there existed in Bavaria another aircraft factory in Bamberg; namely the Messerschmitt Flugzeugbau G. m. b. H. in its initial stages. Because of the excellent results of some of the gliders Willy Messerschmitt had constructed, he had become quite well - known. The experience gained thereby was used by him in a small transport plane for one pilot and four passengers. The contract for this plane was given by Mr. Theo Cronweiss, formerly the Director of the Nordbayerisehen Verkehreflug G. m. b. H.

This type of plane, Model M 18 (license number D 947) was a complete success. It enabled Messerschmitt to negotiate with the Trade Ministry for further subsidies. Because of the unfavorable economic conditions the Trade Ministry did not permit the Bavarian State to support two aircraft factories at the same time; namely, the Bayerische Flugzeugwerke A. G. in Augsburg, and the Messerschmitt Flugzeugbau G. m. b. H. in Bamberg.

Since the travel ministry in Berlin was of the same opinion, both ministries attempted to amalgamate these two airplane factories into one.

Because of his former successes, Messerschmitt by no means wanted to give up his leadership, at least as far as developement was concerned. But finally in the Fall of 1927, after very difficult bickering, an agreement was reached between the Messerschmitt Flugzeugbau in Bamberg and the Bayerische Flugzeugwerke A. G. to merge the two companies under the following conditions:

That the Bayerischen Flugzeugwerke A. G. limit itself only to production of aircraft and then principally to Messerschmitt aircraft, while giving up development completely. On the other hand the Messerschmitt Flugzeugbau G. m. b. H. would limit itself to developement of new types, on which the Bayerische Flugzeugwerke A. G. would have first priority.

Hereby the two firms existed individually whereby their economic effect was that of one firm. The contract was made on September 8, 1927. At this time Diploma Engineer Willy Messerschmitt moved his factory and personnel to Augsburg.

Because of this contract, the mass production of the M 18 B as well as development and manufacturing of the first prototype of M 20 A was started in the Fall of 1927. The M 20 is a transport plane, high wing monoplane, made totally of metal with a BMW VI A motor, carrying ten passengers and two pilots. Besides this, in the course of 1927 two types were developed without Messerschmitt having a hand in it. There were the BFW 1 "Sperber", a training place of composite construction with a Siemens SH 12 motor, and the BFW 3, the "Flamingo" with a steel pipe fuselage.

The first test flight of the M 20 took place on the 26th of February, 1928. In its first flight the plane crashed. The covering had come loose at the rear edge of the wing, which the pilot misjudged to be serious damage. He attempted to bail out despite having only 80 meters altitude. Because of this accident the German Lufthansa Berlin cancelled its contract.

The BFW A. G. immediately built a second prototype which was tested on the second of August, 1928, by Theo Croneiss. The plane proved to be a complete success. So much so that the Deutsche Lufthansa again took interest and ordered production with certain changes.

In the Reichstag the Reich's Travel Ministry was repeatedly attacked because of its ownership of an aircraft factory. So it was finally decided to sell the factory to private owners. Among others interested in the purchase were the companies Ernst Heinkel G. m. b. H., Warnemunde and Albatros Flugzeugwerke, Berlin Johannisthal. Because the Travel Ministry wanted to sell its shares for 100% value, no success was achieved. Messerschmitt who feared losing his independence should the shares be bought by some unknown partner, attempted to find purchasers whom he knew. He succeeded when he persuaded the family Strohmeyer-Raulino, his friends in Bamberg, to buy the afore-mentioned shares. The total of RM 400,000 shares were bought by Strohmeyer-Raulino on the first of July, 1928, from the Bavarian State at 100% value. At this same time the committee of shareholders as well as the management of the factory were newly established. The committee of shareholders as of the 1st of July were as follows:

Mr. Otto Strohmeyer, Bamberg, as Chairman.
Prof. Dr. Paul Rieppel, Munich.
Lawyer. Dr. V. Scancony, Munich.
Ministerialrat. Dr. Hellman, Munich.

Dr. S. C. Ruffer, the former individual manager, had to resign and his place was taken by Fritz Hille and Willy Messerschmitt, as managers. RM 400,000 shares were divided between the group Strohmeyer-Raulino and Messerschmitt as follows:

RM 330,000 Strohmeyer-Raulino
RM 70,000 Willy Messerschmitt

On the first of July, 1928, the whole developing department of the Messerschmitt Flugzeugbau G. m. b. H. was taken over by the BFW A. G. and the contract between the two was voided. The contract was never formally voided because the Messerschmitt Flugzeugbau G. m. b. H. retained ownership of all Messerschmitt patents before and after.

In 1928, the following types were developed:

M 21   A two-seater training B1 plane with composite construction. The first proto-types were tested in the summer of 1928. Mass production of this type did not follow.

M 22   A two-motored mail bi-plane in composite construction with three wing spars. The first prototype was tested in the Spring of 1930. Because one of the blades of the three-bladed propeller broke loose, the plane crashed in the summer of 1930. Further production of this type of plane did not follow.

M 23 a and b   A two-seated private low-wing plane, constructed of wood with any of the following motors: Bristol-Genet, SH 13 a, Argus AS 8, Salmson 40 PS and Cirrus-Hermes. The test flight of the first prototype was in December 1928. The M 23 was produced in a greater number; it found a great use in private circles. In 1929 it won first prize in the first International European contest for private planes.

M 24 a   Because of the great demand for a transport plane for eight passengers, smaller than the M 20 and larger than M 18, this type was developed in all-metal high wing construction. The Junkers L 5 and BMW 5 A motors could be used. Only a few planes of this type were manufactured.

The profit of the factory did not correspond to the extensive activities of the developing department. Even when in 1928, the turnover could be increased by 40%, the profit from the production of the Messerschmitt planes did not cover the expenses so that the turnover finally brought losses. So it was impossible from the very beginning that the development expenses were not covered by the turnover. The factory therefore had to attempt to get the Travel Ministry to cover its development expenses through the so-called development commissions on subsidies. This was achieved once again in 1929, after the balance of 1928 had shown a loss of RM 280,000.

The losses could be balanced by a subsidy of RM 200,000 for the development of each of the following types: M 20, M 21, and M 23. The corporation further reactivated unlisted reserves so that the balance, on the 31st of December, 1928, showed a profit of RM 1600.

In 1929, the economic crisis of BFW A. G. turned from bad to worse. Throughout the whole German aircraft industry, the expenses from the development could only be partly covered by the profit from production. But nowhere were the difficulties so evident as by the BFW A. G. The Travel Ministry therefore decided to give all important firms, such as Junkers, Heinkel, Dornier, Arado, and BFW, a single subsidy primarily to balance the losses caused by the expenses for development.

The BFW A. G. acquired in 1927, a subsidy of RM 700,000 besides its developing contracts. RM 587,000 of this subsidy were consumed already in 1929.

The financial situation of the company in 1929 was still more difficult than in the year before. The foreign capital raised in 1929 had increased to RM 450,000. This sum appears to be unusually high regarding the total capital of the balance in 1929 of about RM 2,000,000; the more so as the increase of the total capital from RM 1,570,000 in 1928 to RM 2,029,000 in 1929, merely was due to the raising of foreign capital, namely short-termed exchange credits. This further increase of foreign capital was merely balanced by the increase of the value of raw materials, prototype construction and design; a very dubious increase of values that still had to prove whether their liquidation would be even possible in the future. The following figures show a comparison between 1928 and 1929 balances.

	ASSETS	
	1928	*1929*
Money Invested in Bldg & Equip.	657,000	676,000
Stock Prototype Construction & Design	528,000	1,196,000
Minor Assemblies	385,000	157,000
Totals	1,570,000	2,029,000

	LIABILITIES	
	1928	*1929*
Own Capital	404,000	406,000
Foreign Capital	1,166,000	1,623,000
Totals	1,570,000	2,029,000

As far as the economic events in 1929 are concerned, it may be of interest that the firm succeeded in that year to draw up license contracts with Estonia, Latvia, and Lithuania, and even to negotiate with the USA. A license contract was drawn up with the Eastern Aircraft Corporation in Pawtucket; this American corporation should get a single license in America for the M 18 and M 26. The contract was drawn up on the following basis:

A) For M 18 Type A. Single Payment of $50,000.
    Payment of $300 to $500 license per plane.
B) For M 26 Type A. Single Payment of $30,000.
    Payment of $150 to $250 license per plane.

During the crash of '29, the EACO ran into financial difficulties that disabled the corporation from starting production. Therefore, RM 200,000 expenses of the BFW A. G., according to a new agreement, were regarded as balanced by a RM 189,000 payment from EACO; the contract thereafter was cancelled.

The developing program started in 1928, was continued in 1929 as follows:

M 18 c

The small transport plane in all-metal construction M 18 b had proved to be a good photographic plane, so according to contracts with Switzerland the plane had to be equipped with a stronger engine as the plane was required to operate with less difficulties in high altitudes. The 220 power motor, Armstrong Siddeley-Lynx, was required. Besides certain reinforcements the M 18 b had to get a higher under carriage to increase the clearance of the propeller. The few planes of this type that had been manufactured were exported to Switzerland and Portugal.

M 18 d

The direction of development, started when the license contract was drawn up with EACO, was continued when the construction of the M18 c was improved to carry five to six passengers and one to two pilots. A new design was made suitable for the 200 horse power Wright Whirlwind motor. This type was an especially good solution. Besides very good results, this plane had especially good flight qualities. It was further acknowledged as a photographic plane.

M 20 b

After the German Lufthansa already had bought two M 20 a planes, it ordered two more planes with certain changes because they previously had been successful. At this time the

Lufthansa began to request a higher stability; therefore, the M 20 a underwent the following changes; Whereas the M 20 a previously had its wings on top of the fuselage, it now was built to blend the high wing with the fuselage. Besides this the plane got an upward dihedral and a sweptback wing. The flight qualities thereby achieved, made this type the most modern German airplane.

M 24 b

As the flight qualities had been improved when M 20 a had been changed to M 20 b the factory therefore attempted to change the M 24 a accordingly. Furthermore, the M 24 b was fitted with stronger motors to use this plane also as a sea plane.

M 26

Owing to the former contract with the EACO, the design and prototype production of a provisional transport high wing plane in all metal construction was started. This type was intended to carry two passengers and one pilot in a closed cabin. The first prototype plane was tested in the Spring of 1930. Only two planes of this type were manufactured. Besides this, the Travel Ministry in 1930 gave the order that this plane was to be developed in an all-electron construction instead of an aluminum alloy. Because of the economic breakdown, more or less, only the design of this electron construction could be carried out while only some minor assemblies were manufactured.

M 23 c

The private plane M 23 b in 1929 won the first prize for Germany in the International European contest. Germany therefore had to manage the contest in the succeeding year.

Therefore according to the regulations set up for the next contest Messerschmitt was ordered to develop a new private plane that should insure victory as far as possible. A private low wing plane in mixed construction, similar to M 23 b, was developed which originally got the number M 27, while it later was finally numbered M 23 c. During the second International European contest this plane stood the test when it won first prize.

M 28

The German Lufthansa had a basic interest in a fast mail plane. Therefore, BFW offered the production of such a plane in a low wing all-metal construction. But only a single plane of this type, M 28 was manufactured with a Pratt-Whitney Hornet motor which was tested in February, 1931. The unfavorable economic situation which already was to be seen by the balance of 1929 went to even worse extremes in 1930. The turnover of the factory was much too small and before all: the expenses of production were larger than the prices finally achieved. The commissions obtained from the Travel Ministry for development covered only an infinitesimal part of the factory's expenses from developing.

In 1929, the subsidies had already been used to a remainder of RM 113,000 so it is no wonder that the factory had a loss of about RM 600,000 by the end of 1930. This loss was kept down to the afore-mentioned figure by an additional subsidy of RM 250,000 from Strohmeyer-Raulino and the reactivation of all unlisted reserves and values to the highest possible degree.

Because of this hopeless situation the commercial manager of the firm, Fritz Hille, decided to take off. He was followed by Franz Ludwig Hebbel, the brother-in-law of the former Minister President of Bavaria, Held. Innumerable discussions with the Travel Ministry and the Bavarian State were without success. At the request of the Travel Ministry the BFW was to enter into negotiations with either the Heinkel G. m. b. H. Warnemunde or Dornier Metalbou G. m. b. H. Friedrisherafen to effect a merger. The terms of these factories were so absolutely inconvenient, that it would have meant the complete abolishment of the BFW. Messerschmitt, for instance, was to be made Chief of the final design department. All these events showed clearly that all the rest of the German Aircraft industry feared that Messerschmitt was becoming a most serious competitor. Therefore, they took the opportunity to either cold-storage him or use his talents for their own purposes and did not shy from making consequent conditions.

Influenced by the rest of the aircraft industry, the Travel Ministry took the same point of view. This is proved by what the Ministerialdirigent Brandenburg said to the representative of the Heinkel firm, V. Pfistermeister, in the lobby of the Reichstag in May, 1931: "Don't mind if the BFW goes bankrupt, it will be less troublesome and less expensive to buy them out."

The opposition gained a point in its favor when the two planes, M 20 b, ordered by the German Lufthansa crashed, one near Dresden, and the other near Breslau, in the Spring 1931. A rupture of the rudder unit and the vertical fin were assumed but not proved. A protracted series of investigations later conducted by the DVL-Berlin, Adlershof, showed, after a whole year, that the formerly assumed load was too small for the gust effect.

Thereupon the German Lufthansa cancelled its order to the BFW for the production of ten M 20 b planes and demanded refund of its down payment. These demands could not be met for production of these planes had already advanced too far.

This incident was the final blow in deciding the BFW crisis, so that no alternative was left but to start the bankruptcy process at the district court in Augsburg on the first of June, 1931. Hereby it became impossible for Messerschmitt personally to continue work for the BFW A.G. An attempt was made to salvage and retain intact as much of the plant's equipment and values as possible to achieve a basis for a new start.

Attorney Konrad Merkel, administrator of the bankruptcy's estate, was enlightened to the fact that starting the company after a certain period of time was the only solution. The Messerschmitt Flugzeugbau G. m. b. H., out of action for some time, now regained some importance. This company proved to be extremely valuable because of its ownership of the Messerschmitt patents, which did not belong to the bankrupt's estate.

The Messerschmitt Flugzeugbau G. b. m. H. had no cash on hand, which made it difficult to effect its reestablishment. The undersigned remembers his proposition to Messerschmitt: that he sell his car in order to obtain the RM 2000 for the first capital of the company. A short time later the license for the M 23 b was sold to Rumania for RM 6000 so that the company had a total of RM 8000 capital in the Fall of 1931.

In cooperation with the administrator of the bankrupt's estate the factory managed to make the German Lufthansa accept the order M 20 and M 28 planes. The Messerschmitt Flugzeugbau G. m. b. H. was ordered to carry out further changes and complete the formerly ordered planes also. In the Fall of 1931, the company was ordered to develop and manufacture a new contest plane for the third International European contest. Messerschmitt thereupon offered the M 29 project. This type made unusual progress in aerodynamic refinement. The outstanding features of this low wing plane of composite construction were landing flaps, undercarriage and an entirely closed cabin. This plane had extraordinarily maximum and minimum speeds but could not be used for the contest, because of two accidents that had happened a short time before the contest started. These accidents were caused by longitudinal stability faults in the airplane. Economically the order for the design and manufacture of the M 29 was an unusual case since it was given at a fixed price. Nevertheless, the Messerschmitt Flugzeugbau G. m. b. H. despite very minute cost calculations by the Travel Ministry achieved excellent profits.

The quarrel between Messerschmitt and the former director of the German Lufthansa,

Erhard Milch, later the General Field Marshal and Secretary of State of the Air Ministry, over the acceptance of the ordered M 20 planes resulted in hard feelings between the two. Milch, in these days, became the strongest opposer of Messerschmitt—a fact which will be referred to later in the story. Besides this, Messerschmitt was on friendly terms with Theo Croneiss, since the time in Bamberg. Croneiss, again, was the strongest competitor of Milch for his company, the Nordbayerischon Verkehraflug G. m. b. H., only demanded RM 0.80 subsidies per kilometer and person, whereas the German Lufthansa demanded RM 2.20 subsidies from the Travel Ministry for the same space and load.

In cooperation with the administrator of the bankrupt estate department it was attempted to end the bankruptcy through a forced agreement. They succeeded in doing so after arrangements had been made with the greater part of the creditors. Ernst Heinkel's firm tried to prevent this agreement, by making a proposition to the city of Augsburg, through the Bavarian Minister President, one of the main creditors, to let the plant and equipment of the BFW to Heinkel. Heinkel guaranteed that he would regulate the number of employees according to the wishes of the city.

These attempts of Heinkel to interfere were frustrated and in a preliminary meeting in December, 1932, the basic agreement between all creditors concerning the forced agreement was reached. The forced agreement was officially testified to at Augsburg district court on 27th of April, 1933. The BFW A. G. could start again and was reopened on the first of May, 1933.

Caused by the two previous years of bankruptcy, the firm naturally had come to a minimum volume. No wonder that the BFW A. G. only had 82 employees in May, 1933.

While the other aircraft factories had managed to survive during the previous hard times, the BFW A. G. was forced to start from scratch. This beginning was not made any easier, for the office in charge of air travel was taken over by Secretary of State Milch after the government had been taken over by the Nazis. Because of his hate for Messerschmitt he certainly had no interest to support the revival of the BFW A. G. Despite this he could not suppress the fact that Messerschmitt had established himself as a leading aircraft designer whom he could not easily eliminate when German air travel was built up.

Nevertheless, Milch did not intend to pay any attention to Messerschmitt's designs at all. He tried to show up Messerschmitt as unimportant and insignificant when he demanded that the factory should only be the manufacturer of other aircraft licenses. The management of the BFW A. G., by all means, wanted to keep the factory alive after the previous quarrels, and therefore could do nothing but yield to the demands.

The whole situation was made more unpleasant by the fact that the BFW A. G. was forced by Milch to manufacture the Heinkel 45 c license plane after Heinkel in the previous years had been the strongest opponent of Messerschmitt and had tried to ruin his reputation.

The Heinkel firm by no means tried to support the license production at the BFW A. G. The representatives of the BFW A. G., who had travelled to Warnemunde to obtain necessary information, the undersigned being among these, could not enter the Heinkel workshop and were not even allowed to see the plane they were supposed to produce. Only after many complaints at the RLM, the Heinkel firm reluctantly gave some information and decided to allow the plane outside of the workshop in an open field. At this time the other German aircraft factories already had extensive commissions for production while BFW A. G. originally was ordered to manufacture twelve He 45 e planes only.

Simultaneously, with the organization of mass production all existing firms got orders for the development of new airplane types. Despite this BFW A. G. did not get any such orders, so that Messerschmitt's very small design department had no important work to do in the Spring of 1933. Therefore, the undersigned travelled to Bucharest in June, 1933, to get a contract for development of a transport plane. A Rumanian aircraft factory finally ordered the design of a high wing transport plane in composite construction for six passengers and two pilots, suitable to be fitted with a Gnome Rhone motor K 14 of 450 horsepower.

Through this contract it was possible to retain a small development department, and prevent the loss of the last few good designers.

The fact that the BFW A. G. got a foreign development commission was used by the former official of the technical office, Major Wimmer (later General) to make serious reproaches to the undersigned and the firm. These complaints were successfully put to an end by the statement that his office had never troubled about giving a development commission, and thereby had forced the company to help itself. This trouble was ended when the RLM finally decided to give the Messerschmitt designing office a contract to develop a new fighter plane.

Since the same contract had already been given to three other German factories; namely, Heinkel, Arado and Focke Wulf. It was clearly defined that no production contracts would follow. This was the order to develop the Me 109 fighter plane.

Besides this, RLM decided at the last minute to partake in the fourth international contest in 1934. Therefore, as well as in the years before, Messerschmitt was ordered to design and manufacture a contest plane according to the conditions already edited for this competition. This private contest plane, Me 108 "Typhoon", was to become a well-known travel plane.

Towards the end of 1933 the BFW A. G. acquired further manufacturing licenses; namely, the order to produce 24 He 45 d and 30 DO 11 additionally. It therefore followed that at the end of 1933, a total of 524 persons were employed.

Still in 1933, Secretary of State Milch demanded that the management of the factory be taken over by someone who appealed to him. The former management of Messerscbmitt and the undersigned did not suit his plans. The BFW was thereby forced to appoint Mr. Schwartskopff as top manager of the factory.

Concerning 1933, it is to be mentioned that the negotiations with the Handley-Page firm in London, that had already been begun in December, 1932, were continued. An agreement was made whereby Messerschmitt sold his single-spar patents for the right to use the Handley-Page slot patent. This agreement was finally signed in 1936.

The difficulty of starting the BFW A. G. from such a small basis, was not apt to guarantee results for the firm in its first year of production.

Nevertheless, the management of the factory was able to start the business of 1934, with the tolerable loss of RM 40,000.

When in 1934, the technical office was taken over by Major Loeb (later General Loeb), a decisive change for the BFW took place. Loeb was one of the few men who showed a deep understanding for the problems of the aircraft industries and an unusual intuition. Loeb, together with Generals Nevor and Kesselring (former official of the economic office of the RLM), were the three big men whom the German Air Travel could thank for its rapid development. All successors were minor personalities and the importance of these three men was never again reached.

Despite serious resistance from the Secretary of State Milch against the BFW A. G., Major Loeb took an absolutely unprejudiced point of view that soon led to close cooperation with Mr. F. W. Seiler, now president of the committee of shareholders.

The rapid enlargement of the whole of the German aircraft industry in these days could clearly be noticed, even at the BFW A. G. The machine factory Epple and Buxbaum was bought up in order to enlarge the territory for production and air fields. It is still in the undersigned's memory, the excitement caused the owners of the factory by this purchase, especially Messerschmitt, personally, who thought that these expenses by no means fitted in with the budget of the firm. The purchase price of Epple and Buxbaum was RM 450,000. It was agreed with the owner of the Bank of Germany that the amount could be divided into nine equal payments of RM 50,000 payable annually. This method of payment thereby made the purchase bearable. Despite this, Messerschmitt then believed that these works would never be used for his purpose and would constitute dead wood as far as the firm was concerned. It was proved in the course of the same year that his opinion was wrong. Not only was the newly purchased firm entirely used in 1934, but a new large production hangar had to be built.

Before Major Loeb succeeded Major Wimmer in his position as official of the technical office, a characteristic episode concerning Messerschmitt had happened clearly bringing to light the prejudices of the RLM. Messerschmitt had been offered a professorship for airplane design at the Technical University in Danzig. Messerschmitt used this occasion to inquire of the RLM if there was any importance attached to his work for aircraft industries in days to come. He was in doubt about this because of the unceasing attacks. Hereupon Major Wimmer let him know that his person would be of no importance for further development of the German air travel, and that, therefore, he would do well to accept the professorship in Danzig. Yet Major Loeb and others around Messerschmitt hindered the fulfillment of this step.

How strong the opposition against Messerschmitt still was was proved when the Me 108 was tested for the European contest. Once again Messerschmitt tried his utmost for technical progress. To achieve the best possible results for lift at low speed flight, he attempted to lengthen the landing flap over the whole extension of the wing and to replace the wing flap by a spoiler. While the first flights were made without difficulties, one of the participants later crashed during a training flight. Hereupon Mr. Osterkamp, manager of the German contest team, incited his fellow contestants Seideman & Morzik to a riotous attitude toward Messerschmitt and his Me 108. Only the intervention by Major Loeb, who incidentally on this day was in Augsburg, could stop these machinations. In the course of the same day, Loeb, accompanied by Mr. Seiler, flew to Berlin to propose to Secretary Milch that Osterkamp should be relieved of his position. Loeb took the correct point of view when he mentioned that during many weeks the plane had previously been tested at the test laboratory in Rechlin (RIM), and that it had been proved faultless. It therefore was not up to Osterkamp to decide whether or not the machine was to be done away with.

Osterkamp's behavior can only be understood by that fact that Milch and his associates thought themselves justified in taking an opposed attitude towards Messerschmitt and his work at every possible opportunity.

The major part of mass production in 1934 still had to be licenses of other firms. Out of all their own designs, merely six Me 108's were manufactured. The development department was entirely wrapped up in design and prototype production of the Me 109. Towards the end of 1934, the design of the Me 110 was started.

Economically, the BFW was able to solidify its investments during 1934. The turnover which had been RM 166,000 in 1933 increased to RM 2,616,000 in 1934.

The main feature of 1935 was the extensive enlargement of space for mass production. In this year the BFW had the following production contracts:

32	Me 108 b	90	Arado 66
35	He 50	115	Go 145
70	He 45 d	10	Me 109

The basis for mass production had to be enlarged to master such an extensive program. The most important building operation was the establishment of hangar 4, which was erected at a distance of two kilometers from the airfield.

These intensive activities on building operations naturally necessitated the continual raising of new credits for investments. The banking houses in these days hesitatingly gave further credit for building operations. Therefore, it was impossible to make the acquisition of money on the private market keep up with the swift progress of the factories expansion. This state of affairs was smoothed out by the investment credits of the RLM even though they were redeemable at any date. Toward the end of 1935, the BFW A. G. had borrowed such a credit totaling RM 3.6 million from the RLM.

The most important event in 1935 was the test flight of the Me 109 prototype which took place toward the end of November.

The progressive economic improvement from 1933 to 1945 can be seen in the following table which lists four important values:

a) the total balance

b) value of money invested (buildings, machinery, equipment, etc.)

c) the turnover

d) the number of employees

IMPORTANT NUMBERS FOR THE ENLARGEMENT OF MTT. A. G. IN AUGSBURG

Date per 31 Dec	Fixed Assets	Total Balance in RM 10000	Total Turnover in RM 10000	Total Turnover for Export	Number of Employees
1933	600	1,505	166	- - -	524
1934	1,520	6,711	2,616	- - -	1,414
1935	3,167	14,182	8,224	- - -	2,403
1936	6,847	32,044	12,099	121	5,182
1937	12,262	56,668	27,550	909	3,439
1938	10,156	68,078	41,876	1,675	6,491
1939	10,821	109,657	84,518	18,595	8,797
1940	12,053	143,880	101,964	17,854	9,809
1941	13,140	225,565	147,500	14,600	11,591
1942	14,800	323,103	102,000	30,600	11,545
1943	15,293	349,908	225,830	65,478	16,298
1944	29,248	- - - -	250,000	- - -	21,171
31 March 1945	- - -	- - -	- - -	- - -	27,263

The total balance shows the year-to-year enlargement of the whole firm. The total of fixed assets shows the value of money invested in buildings, and equipment at the end of each year. The depreciation was already written off. Despite a large expansion the management of the firm always succeeded in keeping the value of fixed assets at a low rate by extensive depreciation, which may be recognized by the comparison between this and total balance.

Year by year the turnover points out the increase of the production volume.

Because of the 3.6 million marks credit which had been raised in 1935, the RLM now

177

demanded that the capital of the firm be increased to RM 400,000. The RLM made a proposal to the effect that this credit should be changed into share capital, whereby the shares naturally have become state property. This would have meant that the BFW A. G. would have been turned over to new owners undeservedly.

Thereby a signal was given to the BFW to frustrate this attempt of the Reich to get the major part of the shares. Tedious discussions led to the so-called consortial agreement with the RLM. According to this agreement the capital was increased by 3.6 million marks to a total of 4 million marks on the 31st of March, 1936. A condition was accepted to the effect that 2.1 million mark shares be administered by a trustee appointed by both sides. Mr. F. W. Seiler, now president of the committee of shareholders, was appointed to this trusteeship. He was, simultaneously, the administrator of the Raulino group shares and the shares of the banking house Carlo Z. Thomsen, totaling RM 500,000, which latter shares had been acquired when share capital was increased through Mr. Seiler's partnership. This administration guaranteed that the Reich could never come in a position to rule over the original shareholders. This agreement had further conditions that the Reich was obliged to sell its shares to original shareholders only, at a fixed price and within the following ten years.

Soon after this increase of capital, the RLM demanded a new expansion of the production basis. Considerations were made by the BFW A. G. as to the means of preventing a new supply of investment subsidies given by the RLM. Further space for production purposes was acquired in Regensburg and a new personal company, the Messerschmitt G. m. b. H. was formed on the 24th of July 1936. The plan to enlarge production facilities in Regensburg was promoted by the refusal of the city of Augsburg to agree with the same plans in the Augsburg district.

Beside seven 108's and three 109's, the factory was mainly engaged in license production in 1936. And yet the production figures of the Me 108, 109, and 110 steadily increased during that year.

In 1937, enormous building operations were carried out at the BFW A. G.; namely, enlargement of hangars 1 and 2 for production, new erection of a large building for the administration and design departments, building up of hangars 3 and 4. The manufacturing of the Me 108 was handed over to the Regensburg shadow factory which began to work toward the end of 1937. This illustrates the great speed with which the Regensburg factory was erected within one year after it had been established on the 24th of July, 1936. It may be mentioned that the plant was absolutely new and no previously existing roads and buildings had been taken over.

In April, 1937, the first flight of the twin-motored Destroyer Me 110 was made. In the summer of 1937, important events occurred at the International Contest Dudendorf by Zurich. During this contest the Me 109 was for the first time shown to the public. It won the following three first-prizes:

1. the speed race
2. the climbing speed contest
3. the military patrol contest

After the successes of the Messerschmitt planes had established his fame during the previous years, the production in 1938 dealt only with Messerschmitt-type planes for the first time. At the same time mass production of Messerschmitt planes was started at a series of other German aircraft factories.

Because of these successes the owners, on the 11th of July, 1938, named the firm Messerschmitt A. G., and simultaneously appointed Prof. Messerschmitt Chairman of the

Managing Committee and General Director. Up to this time all the patents were owned by the Messerschmitt and Co. KG, which was owned by Messerschmitt only. On the 5th of August, an agreement was made with this firm making all existing patents the property of the Messerschmitt A. G. The money paid for these patents to the Messerschmitt and Co. KG was used to buy up the shares of the Reich.

The design of the Me 210 was begun in the fall of 1938.

The extensive enlargements, which had led to an increase in capital in 1936, now necessitated anew the clearing up of the short-term investment credits. Therefore, the RLM was enlightened to the fact that a great number of expenses due to air raid precautions, for instance the dispersals of the several buildings, immediately be depreciated. Tedious negotiations with the RLM and the Reich's finance court finally led to the approval of a special depreciation. By the agreement on the 12th of July, 1939, a single depreciation totaling seven million marks was granted to the Messerschmitt A. G. A short-term investment credit of eight million marks was replaced by a credit given by the Bavarian Vereinsbank Munich. Out of these eight million marks, five million marks were paid back in 1940 and three million marks changed into loan on mortgage termed for ten years.

Production of Me 109 was handed over to the Regensburg factory, along with the Me 108 in 1939. Production of the Me 110 was started in Augsburg in great numbers. More than 537 Me 110's were manufactured in Augsburg before the end of 1939.

The production of the Me 109 and the Me 110 was carried out simultaneously by eight other German aircraft factories in 1939.

In order to judge the development in aerial warfare it is important to know that the first design of Me 262 was already begun on the first of April, 1939. The project was offered to the RLM for the first time on the 7th of June, 1939. On the 19th of December, 1939, the first inspection of the mock-up by the representatives of the RLM was carried out. Meanwhile the building operations at the Regensburg factory were mainly finished by the end of 1939. Therefore, final agreements had to be made concerning the short-term investment credits between the RLM and this company. Because this company from its very beginning had been established with the intention to avoid further loans for the Messerschmitt A. G. in Augsburg, an agreement was made with the RLM to increase the capital of the company from RM 20,000 to seven million marks. The rest of the whole eight million marks investment credits remained loaned to the Air Travel Bank.

Because of its previous merits during the establishment of this factory, the Messerschmitt A. G., by an optional contract, was enabled to either partially or totally buy up the Messerschmitt G. m. b. H. shares in the course of the following ten years.

The Me 210 prototype was tested on the 1st of September, 1939.

The Reich's last shares of the Messerschmitt A. G. were bought back in the spring of 1940. Thereby private ownership was totally reestablished for the Augsburg parent company.

The profits of 1940 were used mainly for consolidation and expansion of the Messerschmitt A. G. In Kematen, near Innsbruck (Tyrol) a small factory was purchased in March, 1940. This factory was made independent and became Messerschmitt G. m. b. H. through the contract on the 13th of June, 1941. Furthermore the Leichtbau G.m.b.H. Regensburg shares and the Pa. Uher & Co. Munich shares were bought in 1940.

After the beginning of the war on the 1st of September, 1939, the turnover increased from 84 million marks in 1939 to 102 million marks in 1940. Regarding the turnover it is worth mentioning that already in 1938 an unusually high turnover was achieved in foreign countries, totaling 80 million marks, as well as in 1940.

Besides the development and testing of the Me 210, which was in full swing in 1940, the question arose, how to transport a 22-ton tank through the air to England in the event of an invasion. Hereupon Messerschmitt made the proposal to transport this tank by means of a gigantic glider. The project was accepted on the 7th of November 1940. Development and mass production were immediately started in special workshops at Leipheim and Obertraubling. The first Me 321 was already tested on the 25th of February, 1941, in Leipheim.

The main part of production lay in the Me 210 and Me 321 planes. Considerable difficulties ensued by a great number of changes hindered the mass production of the Me 210.

The only event of importance in 1941 was the increase of the four million marks capital by 40 percent, so that by the 1st of January, 1942, the capital totalled 5,600,000 marks. Because of a new law dealing with the A. G. investments, certain unlisted capital changed into share capital.

The first flight of the Me 262, on the 4th of April,(sic) constituted another important event in 1941. The plane was not yet equipped with a Junkers TL jet unit; instead a Junkers Jumo 210 G was built into the nose to test the flight abilities.

In the summer of 1941 the Messerschmitt A.G. along with bank of Seiler & Co. brought back the Eiso-Schrauben G. m. b. H. firm and a further agreement was made with the Ungarischen Armarturenfabrik in Budapest resulting in the purchase of 25% of the shares of this factory.

After the first planes of Me 210 mass production were handed to Air Force units, a series of accidents occurred, so that the whole production of this type was finally stopped on the 17th of April 1942. This order was one of the most insensible and serious measures ever taken by the RLM. This order caused many workers to be without proper employment for many months, and the waste of a high value of materials and minor assemblies. It finally effected a loss of at least 600 planes of the total output of the German aircraft production.

The bad qualities of the Me 210 in a side slip could be improved by the installation of slots. The first plane that was changed was ready to fly in the beginning of July. Despite this, it was only towards the end of 1942 that the RLM decided to start mass production anew on a smaller basis and with a new official number Me 410.

The expenses caused by the order to stop, in Augsburg as well as for other Me 210 producing factories, amounted to a total of 30 million marks.

Meanwhile, in the Leipheim shadow factory, motors were fitted to the Me 321 glider plane, and the production of the large transport plane, Me 323 was begun.

The Obertraubling factory was attached to the Messerschmitt G. m. b. H. in Regensburg.

Due to Me 210 stop-orders the 1942 turnover went down from 147 million marks in 1941 to 102 million marks, and the number of employees decreased from 15,100 to 12,800 persons. Simultaneously with the Me 210 stop-overs the hatred between Milch and Messerschmitt again became very evident. Milch at once demanded of Messerschmitt that he immediately resign from his position as general director and general manager. He was then succeeded by the chairman of the committee of shareholders, Theo Croneiss. Because of this stuffy atmosphere, the big event of the first flight of the Me 262 with two Junkers TL jet units 004 on the 17th of July (sic) 1942 went by completely unobserved. Because of the general agitation incited anew against Messerschmitt, no official recognition was given to this very important event. It was only on the 19th of May 1943 after General Gallands' personal test, that the plane was officially acknowleged for the first time. Because of Galland's recommending report, the RLM was forced to the more favorable decision.

On the 15th of July, 1943, the Messerschmitt A. G. made the offer to the RLM to start Me 262 production at a rate of 60 planes per month starting in January, 1944. This proposal contained all suppositions necessary to accomplish such a program. The manufacture of jigs

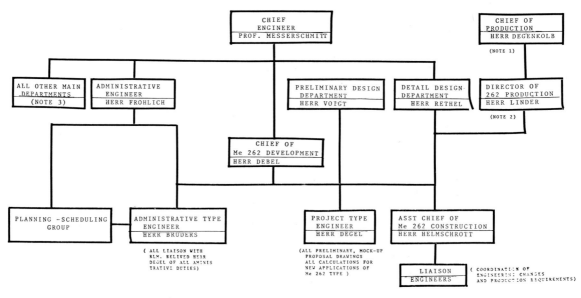

(1) THE GERMAN-WAR PRODUCTION MINISTRY ASSIGNED HERR DEGENKOLB TO CONTROL AND SUPERVISE PRODUCTION ALL MESSERSCHMITT TYPES. (4) HERR DEGENKOLB TOOK OVER THIS POSITION ABOUT FEB. 1st 1945, SUCCEEDING SEVERAL PREVIOUS APPOINTEES, ALL OF WHOM FAILED TO SATISFY THE GOVERNMENTS REQUIREMENTS.

(2) HERR LINDER IN REALITY WAS IN CHARGE OF ALL MESSERSCHMITT PRODUCTION, AND CARRIED FULL RESPONSIBILITY FOR ALL Me 262 PRODUCTION, ALTHOUGH HE HAD NOT YET BEEN APPOINTED CHIEF OF PRODUCTION FOR THE MESSERSCHMITT COMPANY.

(3) THIS GROUP INCLUDES ALL OTHER MAIN DEPARTMENTS SERVING IN A CONSULTING CAPACITY TO HERR DEGEL, SUCH AS STRUCTURES, FLIGHT TESTING,PROTOTYPE PRODUCTION, SERVICES, ENGINEERING, ETC.

(4) WHICH INCLUDED ALSO CONTROL OF ENGINEERING.

Organization Chart of development staff for Me 262

and tools was an especially critical part of the program after the lack of manhours for these purposes had already become evident, when previous programs were proposed. Yet the RLM promised to terminally take care of the factories' needs especially concerning personnel. Despite the promise of 1,800 workers for the jig and tool production, these men were so late that the jig and tool department lost 2.8 million manhours within nine months. Besides this, the greater part of assembly fixtures and acceptance gauges of the fuselage was demolished during the first air raid on Regensburg on the 17th of August 1943.

The firm's difficulties were multiplied by the increasing superiority of the Allied Air Force, and therefore an attack on the Augsburg factory had to be reckoned with. The dispersal of the Augsburg factory was begun in the Fall of 1943. First of all, the whole development department was transferred to Oberammergau in October 1943. From their very beginning, the plans concerning the mass production of the Me 262 were to begin manufacturing, not only in Augsburg, but in many different places. On the 25th of February 1944 the first air raid on Augsburg was made, as had been expected, but no damage was done to the Me 262 production after it had been removed from the city.

In the beginning of March the aircraft production program was taken over by the Speer Ministry. Therefore, on the 1st of March, 1944, a commissioner, Ganamtsleiter Prof. Overlash, was attached to the Augsburg factory. From this time on, the factory's management was practically put out of action because direct orders were issued by this new office.

This state of affairs turned even worse when commissioner and sponsors were appointed for new type of planes, along with the general trustee, Director Degenkolb, who was assigned on the 1st of February 1945.

Under the management of the Speer Ministry, the Me 262 program was enormously enlarged, owing to the fact that the Me 262's importance was now realized, regretfully one year too late. First of all, the Speer Ministry set up a staff in order to increase the number of fighter planes, the so-called Jaegerstab. This staff appeared to be successful during the first two months, since it could rely on its former connections with the armament ministry. But when the Jaegerstab was extended to the whole German armament industry it very soon lost its efficiency and activity. The promises of the Speer Ministry to fulfill the suppositions previously demanded by the firm were not taken care of. Mr. Saur would not allow discussion about these things. He even went so far as to claim that the Ministry had done all that was possibly in its power, despite the open facts. Mr. Saur was in the habit of abruptly curtailing discussions, whenever the question arose as to whether these demands of the firm had been completely ignored or only partially fulfilled. Yet these demands had been checked and agreed upon by the armament Ministry. The consequences were that the output did not come up to par with the planned progress. The firm was continually made responsible for the mistakes the ministry did not want to admit. Therefore, as already mentioned, special mandates, sponsors, special commissioners and general trustees were appointed. A general mix-up of institutions, rapidly following each other, was created, which automatically threatened to destroy the firm's organization.

Regretfully, Mr. Saur's staff consisted of a great number of people who had not the slightest idea of aircraft manufacturing. Mr. Lange, for instance, the official of the department for airplane production, was no expert in this line, and therefore never could judge the importance of the difficulties that arose. Urged by his superior, Mr. Saur, he used to make promises during negotiations which finally could not be kept. Besides, problems became more serious day by day toward the end of 1944. Caused by heavy attacks by the Allied Air Force on the German lines of communication, it became more and more difficult to get the necessary raw materials for the increasing numbers of production. Despite a general lack of gasoline or diesel oil, a continuously increasing number of trucks had to be used as a means of transportation.

Besides this, the steady advance of the allied troops brought about the continual transfer of materials and production facilities, which in turn necessitated further means of transportation. The Speer Ministry never showed any understanding that the increasing transportation program had to cause production losses. It always demanded that the transfer of whole plants be carried out without a decrease of production. When, by the end of February 1945, the Speer Ministry, especially Mr. Saur, had not obtained the desired results, despite all threats of serious penalties for the factory's management, the Me 262 program was finally handed over to SS-Obergruppenfuhrer Kammler.

Now that the situation of the aircraft industry came to its worst, this group of men had even fewer experts at its disposal than its predecessors. No one was able to judge the arising difficulties and despite all threats a basis for a reasonable production could not be regained.

From March 1945 onward, one event followed another so closely that there was no more regular production. The continual transfers of dispersals from place to place practically reduced the firm to transportation activities.

Despite all these gigantic problems a total of 1,443 Me 262's were delivered between March 1944 and the 20th of April 1945. These extraordinary results could be achieved only by the all-out activities of all the personnel and workmen of the Messerschmitt factory. These men did their utmost when they worked more than 70 hours per week to manufacture this number of planes.

These activities were brought to a rapid end when the Allied troops occupied Bavaria and the Messerschmitt factories towards the end of April, 1945.

S/ R. KOKOTHAKI

Messerschmitt Financial Condition

By: Lawrence D. Bell, Bell Aircraft, ATI, USSTAF

Individuals Interrogated:
F. W. Seiler, President and Chairman of the Board of Messerschmitt; and Mr. W. H. Stromeyer, Administrative Assistant to Willy Messerschmitt

Place:
Oberammergau, Germany
Date:
22 July 1945

This interrogation had solely to do with the financial aspects of the Messerschmitt Company, Mr. Seiler answering most of the questions and Mr. Stromeyer acting as interpreter. They reported the Messerschmitt Company to be the only privately owned airplane manufacturing company in Germany and that they had had many bitter fights with the government over the past many years to provide some form of nationalization. The Company is owned entirely by six (6) stockholders of which Willy Messerschmitt is one, owning about 35%. The other stockholders are a matter of record in other reports. The following information on volume of business and profit and number of employees, etc., was furnished:

	Volume in Marks	Profit in Marks	Profit After Taxes	% of Profit on Sales Before Taxes	After Taxes	No. of Employees
1944	250,000,000	Audit	Not Available			27,263
1943	255,000,000	15,431,000	4,562,000	6.0	1.6	23,787
1942	102,000,000	3,100,000	715,000	3.0	0.7	18,070
1941	147,000,000	7,800,000	1,500,000	5.3	1.0	13,487
1940	101,964,000	11,600,000	700,000	10.9	0.7	9,809
1939	84,518,000	7,558,000	379,000	8.8	0.4	8,797
1938	41,880,000	1,781,000	322,000	4.2	0.8	6,491

Apparently the Company declined contracts on fixed price basis after 1941 or 1942 because the difficulties of operating under war conditions rendered cost estimating inaccurate. Seiler claimed that the firm made a profit of 6% on sales under cost plus contracts, the prices always being adjusted to this percentage of profit. Taxes were 60% until 1943 and 1944 when they were negotiated upward to a figure of from 70% to 80%. The Government accountants kept a close audit of costs and apparently the financial operations were closely controlled. All operations of Messerschmitt apparently were privately financed. In the past few years the Company negotiated a 25 year loan for 100,000,000 marks from insurance companies, paying slightly over 4% interest which Messerschmitt considered a very favorable rate. This loan was secured by the assets of the Corporation and was intended to be sufficient to cover the costs of all expansion of buildings, land, machinery and equipment and three (3) months supply of raw materials. There remains unpaid on this loan as of now about 95,000,000 marks. In addition, the firm borrowed, on short term loans, a total of some 250,000,000 marks from three (3) banking firms at an interest rate of 5% which Seiler said was 1% before (sic) the market. Apparently the insurance companies and banks preferred to loan money to Messerschmitt rather than buy war bonds because of the higher interest rate, and in recent months it was considered to be better security.

APPENDIX **G**

Glossary of German Terms

Note: Some German terms are used in the text for authenticity, because English translation often does not convey precisely the same meaning. This glossary is intended to provide a translation of those terms, and to sort out the distinctions that might otherwise clutter the text.

1. *Ergaenzungsjagdgeschwader*
   A replacement training unit which is part of a larger operational Jagdgeschwader. The Germans could not afford the luxury of a standard training program similar to that enjoyed by U.S.A.A.F., and were sometimes forced to under take operations and training simultaneously.

2. *Erprobungskommando*
   A test detachment which combined service test evaluations of the aircraft with pilot training, and on occasion, operational missions.

3. *Flettner*
   An auxiliary moveable portion of a main control surface used for reducing control forces, or for trimming, named for its inventor.

4. *Fuhrerraum*
   Cockpit.

5. *Führer-Befehl*
   Refers to a directive from Hitler which emphasized his intention to use the Me 262 for bombing operations, issued June 8, 1944, and rescinded November 4th.

6. *General der jagdflieger*
   General of the Fighter Forces, a position held by *Generalleutnant* Adolf Galland until he fell from Goering's favor.

7. *Generalleutnant*
   Lieutenant General (equivalent to Major General in U.S.A.A.F.)

8. *Generalmajor*
   Major General (equivalent to Brigadier General in U.S.A.A.F.)

9. *Gruppe*
   A unit consisting of three *Staffeln*:

10. *Hauptmann*
    Captain.

185

11. *Jabo*

German diminutive for fighter bomber, from Jagd bomber.

12. *Jagdgeschwader*

Fighter wing, normally comprising from 108 to 144 aircraft (although usually not actually up to this strength) and consisting of three *Gruppen* (Groups) plus a staff element.

13. *Jagdverband 44*

Jagdverband (Fighter Formation) 44 was a special unit consisting of elite pilots which fought on with the Me 262 until May 3, 1945.

14. *Kampfgeschwader*

A bomber group.

15. *Ketten*

A prewar fighter formation consisting of a three aircraft element, and reverted to by JV 44's Me 262 because it simplified formation turns.

16. *Oberfeldwebel*

Rank equivalent to U. S. A. A. F. Master Sergeant.

17. *Oberst*

Rank equivalent to U. S. A. A. F. Colonel.

18. *Reichsluftfahrtministerium* (RLM)

State Air Ministry.

19. *Reichsmarschall*

Unique title bestowed on Herman Goering to give him higher military rank than all other German officers.

20. *Schwalbe*

"Swallow", Me 262 fighter nickname.

21. *Schwarm*

A four plane element, three of which made up a Staffel.

22. *Staffel*

A basic organizational element roughly equivalent to a squadron.

23. *Sturmvogel*

"Stormbird", the Me 262 fighter bomber nickname.

24. *Turbos*

A nickname for jet powered aircraft.

25. *Volksjaeger*

"Peoples fighter", the nickname for the Heinkel He 162 jet fighter.

26. *Volkstrum*

"Peoples Army" a militia type army formed late in the war from civil resources.

Bibliography

1. Bowers, P.M., and Swanborough, G., *United States Military Aircraft Service 1908,* London, Putnam and Company Limited, 1971.

2. Boyne, Walter J. and Lopez, Donald S., Editors *The Jet Age,* Smithsonian Institution Press, 1979.

3. Galland, Adolf, *The First And The Last,* New York, Henry Holt and Company, 1959.

4. Green, William, *The Warplanes of The Third Reich,* Garden City, New York, Doubleday and Company Inc., 1972.

5. *Warplanes of the Second World War Fighters,* Volume 2, London, Macdonald Co., 1961.

6. Merrick, Kenneth H., *Messerschmitt Me 262 Described,* Victoria, Australia, 1972.

7. Price, Alfred, *Luftwaffe Handbook, 1934-1935,* New York, Charles Scribner & Sons, 1977.

8. Smith, J. R., Kay, A. and Creek, E.J., *German Aircraft of World War 2,* London, Putnam, 1970.

9. Speer, Albert, *Inside the Third Reich,* New York, The MacMillan Company, 1970.

10. Steinhoff, Johannes, *The Last Chance,* London, Hutchinson and Company, 1977.

11. Thetford, Owen, *Aircraft of the Royal Air Force Since 1918,* New York, Funk & Wagnalls, 1968.

12. Toliver R. Ford Constable, T.J., Fighter Aces of the Luftwaffe, Fallbrook, CA., Aero Publishers, Inc. 1977.

13. Zeigler, Mano, *Turbinen Jager Me 262,* Stuttgart Verlag, 1977.

CHART ONE

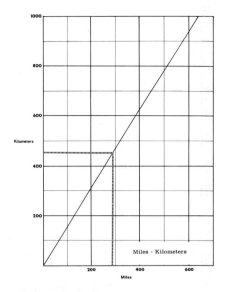

MILES - KILOMETERS

EXAMPLE:
ENTER CHART AT 280 MPH
GO UP TO LINE,
READ ON LEFT SCALE 450
KILOMETERS PER HOUR

(THIS SAME CHART CAN BE
 USED FOR DISTANCES.)

CHART TWO

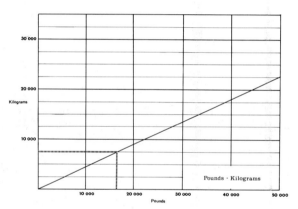

POUNDS - KILOGRAMS

EXAMPLE:
ENTER CHART AT 16.500 POUNDS
GO UP TO LINE AND READ ON
LEFT SCALE 7500 KGS

CHART THREE

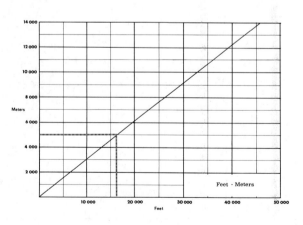

FEET - METERS

EXAMPLE:
ENTER CHART AT 5000 METERS
READ RIGHT TO LINE,
GO DOWN TO BOTTOM SCALE
AND READ 16,400 FEET